ROSALBA'S JOURNAL

And Other Papers

HORACE WALPOLE

(FROM THE PORTRAIT BY ROSALBA)

ROSALBA'S JOURNAL

And Other Papers

By

AUSTIN DOBSON

Avtant icy qv'aillevrs

Essay Index Reprint Series

BOOKS FOR LIBRARIES PRESS
FREEPORT, NEW YORK

First Published 1915
Reprinted 1970

PR 4606
R6

STANDARD BOOK NUMBER:
8369-1605-0

LIBRARY OF CONGRESS CATALOG CARD NUMBER:
71-111827

PRINTED IN THE UNITED STATES OF AMERICA

TO

COL. W. F. PRIDEAUX, C.S.I.

DEAR COL. PRIDEAUX,

    The first of these papers—you will see—was written at your suggestion; and this, I am reminded, is by no means my sole obligation to your varied and accurate knowledge of the Century in which we are both so keenly interested. Will you therefore accept the dedication of the present volume?

        Yours sincerely,

          AUSTIN DOBSON.

*** *This Dedication was accepted by Col. Prideaux; but his death took place before the publication of the book.*

CONTENTS

ILLUSTRATIONS

ROSALBA'S JOURNAL

AMONG the many treasures of Horace
Walpole's Long Gallery at Strawberry
Hill was a portrait of John Law of Lauriston,
the 'inventor of the Mississippi-scheme.' It was
drawn by the once-celebrated Venetian pastellist,
ROSALBA CARRIERA; and hung—we are told—
in a niche to the left of the chimney-piece, above
the Boccapadugli eagle found 'within the pre-
cinct of Caracalla's baths at Rome.' Looking to
the fugitive character of the method employed
by the artist, Walpole had prudently placed it
under glass; and for greater security, had fixed it
firmly to a carved network—'shaking' (he apolo-
getically explained to an antiquary who proposed
to borrow it) 'being very prejudicial to crayons.'
He regarded it as 'one of the best of Rosalba's
works'; and an excellent likeness, since it
closely resembled Law's daughter, whom he knew
well, though he could never have seen her father.
It must have been painted at Paris late in 1720,
not long before Law quitted France for ever.
But how it got to the Twickenham museum;
and what became of it when, at the sale of 1842,

B

it was bought by '— Brown, Esq., Pall Mall,' for £15 15s., is now difficult to determine. Possibly it has succumbed to some of the 'shakings' so perilous to its diuturnity.[1]

The Law portrait, however, was not Walpole's solitary specimen of Rosalba. His catalogues reveal a 'Group of Heads . . . for the story of Diana and Callisto,' a 'Girl with Flowers,' and a portrait of Robert Walpole, second Earl of Orford, 'painted in water-colours . . . with all the force of oil.' Then there is a picture 'in crayons' of Lady Sophia Fermor, Lord Pomfret's eldest daughter, 'drawn as Juno'; and another (glazed) of Walpole's friend, Francis Seymour Conway, Earl of Hertford. But the most notable collection of Horace's friends is disclosed (with some auction-room incoherency) in the 1842 catalogue as 'Lot I [Twenty-first Day's Sale]. Six curious and interesting sketches, drawn at Venice, Portraits of the Earl of Lincoln, Horace Walpole, John Chute, Joseph Spence, Mr. Chaloner [?] and Mr. Whitdsend [?], by ROSALBA.'

Oddly enough, most of these persons figure together in Walpole's 'Short Notes of My Life,' under date of 1741. In May of that year, he

---

[1] There is, or was, an 'unfaithful' copy of it at Versailles (Sensier).

says, Gray, who had hitherto been his travelling
companion on the Grand Tour, quitted him at
Reggio (this was the occasion of the well-known
misunderstanding), going to Venice with Francis
Whithed (disguised above as ' Mr. Whitdsend ')
and John Chute. Then Walpole fell ill, and re-
covering went Venice-ward himself, accompanied
by Joseph Spence, Professor of Poetry, and Henry
Clinton, Earl of Lincoln, with whom he subsequently travelled home as far as Paris. This accounts for five of the portraits. ' Mr. Chaloner,'
the sixth, is unknown to the Walpole Correspondence, though ' Chaloner' was a name of
the Chute family. But Francis Whithed figures
frequently in the letters; and as for John Chute,
' of the Vyne in Hampshire,' was he not later,
with Mr. Pitt of Boconnoc, part-designer of the
mantelpiece in the Long Gallery? To Spence of
the ' Anecdotes '—that amiable ' silver penny of
a man '—with his pupil Lord Lincoln, belong
the credit of saving Walpole's life after Gray had
parted from him. They found him ' scarce able
to speak' with quinsy; and it was due to Spence's
promptly summoning Dr. Antonio Cocchi from
Florence that he got better and accompanied his
preservers to Venice. Here, no doubt, Walpole's
portrait was drawn with the others; and it must

have been either the first sketch or a replica of
the head in a laced hat and domino, assigned to
Rosalba, and familiar in his works.[1] All the six
sketches were purchased in 1842 for a trifling
sum by a member of the Cholmondeley family.

It has been said by a great authority that one
should never have a porch to one's essay. But
the foregoing particulars derive their justification
from the fact that M. Alfred Sensier's very valuable 'Journal de Rosalba Carriera pendant son
Séjour à Paris en 1720 et 1721' (1865), which
forms the subject of this paper, although furnished
with notes largely in excess of the text, and but-
tressed by a bulky 'Notice Biographique,' refrains
from mentioning them at all, and makes but
meagre reference to 'Walpoole' himself. M. Sensier, however, is able to assure us, on the faith of
the Venetian archives, that his heroine (who

---

[1] A pastel portrait of Horace Walpole by Rosalba,
answering to this description, is at present on loan at the
Fine Art Gallery, Brighton. Its owner is Mr. T. H. Vade-
Walpole, and it formerly belonged to Walpole himself.
We are indebted for this information to the courtesy of
the Director of the Brighton Public Library, Mr. Henry
D. Roberts. Rosalba's picture of Whithed—'a fine young
personage in a coat all over spangles'—is said to be at the
Vyne (Chaloner Chute's 'History of the Vyne,' 1888, pp.
100, 101).

seems to have been reticent about her age) was
the eldest daughter of Andrea Carriera and his
wife, Alba di Angela Foresti; and that, according to the registers of the church of SS. Gervasio
e Protasio in Venice, she was born at Chioggia,
or Chiozza, on 7 October 1675. She was christened Rosa Alba—names which, following the
Italian fashion, she afterwards liquefied into
Rosalba.[1] Her family, though poor, was respectable. Her grandfather, Antonio Pasqualino, was
a painter; and of her two younger sisters, who
eventually became her pupils and assistants, one
married another painter, Antonio Pellegrini,
whose artistic function it was to decorate immense surfaces of ceiling with extraordinary
facility and despatch, acquiring a reputation to
which, M. Sensier says rather ambiguously, 'Time
has done justice.' From her father, who had
been a soldier and a local official, she inherited
nothing but a taste for drawing and an excellent
handwriting. His earnings from all sources did
not suffice to support his family, and his wife had
to labour as a lace-worker, producing that hand-
made Venice point now so priceless. Rosalba

[1] A complimentary sonnet in Italian by Pierre-Jean
Mariette of the 'Abecedario' is addressed to her as
Ros'alba Carriera.

began to design early, copying her father's
sketches and drawing patterns for her mother's
lace—a task in those days not disdained by artists
of repute. But taste changed, and Venice point
went out of fashion. As a more profitable pursuit
the young girl turned to the embellishment of
snuff-box lids, an art in which she speedily became expert. From snuff-box ornamentation she
passed to miniature—a still more congenial task.
Antonio Lazzari, the engraver Diamantini, and
Balestra are named among the masters who found
in her the aptest of pupils. Her more ambitious
efforts were materially influenced by the work of
Pietro Liberi, whose system, like that of Balestra,
consisted in combining the excellences of many
masters—a course which, if it suppressed initia-
tive and originality, seems to have been singularly
lucrative. Rosalba also adventured in oil, one of
her efforts in this way being a portrait of that
handsome Elector of Saxony, afterwards Augustus
III, King of Poland, who remained her lifelong
friend and patron. But her staple production was
miniature, which from 1700 onwards engrossed
her attention and kept her fully employed, until
the minute application it entailed began to warn
her not to overtax her eyesight. At this point it
was that she turned her thoughts almost exclu-

sively to pastel, which, though already a practised art, especially for preparatory studies, had
not found too many practitioners. In oil-painting
the field was crowded with formidable competitors; but the less popular pastel, with its
brilliant contrasts and silvery transparencies, its
vivid tints and velvety softness, offered special
facilities for the display of Rosalba's gifts as well
as the disguise of her deficiencies. Her essays in
oil and her ability as a miniaturist, moreover,
were of service to her in working with coloured
chalks; and she speedily came to be saluted by
the liberal laudation of her countrymen as the
'prima pittrice' of Europe. She was admitted in
1703 as a member of the Clementina of Bologna,
and in 1705 of the Academy of St. Luke at Rome.
Her diploma picture was warmly welcomed by
the octogenarian ' prince of the Academy,' Carlo
Maratti, and was apparently exhibited by Ghezzi,
the secretary, to Pope Clement XI.

By this time Rosalba's position as a miniature-
painter and pastellist was permanently established,
and she had only to maintain her connection with
her different patrons in Germany and Italy. By
and by, her sister Angela, as already related, became the wife of Antonio Pellegrini; but Giovanna,
or Giovannina, also an accomplished miniaturist,

remained her pupil and assistant. After the date
of her admission to the Roman Academy there is
little to record but progress. The chief events of
the next few years are : first, her acquaintance with
John Law of Lauriston, then, in consequence of
his fatal duel with the cryptic ' Beau ' Wilson,
a fugitive from England subsisting precariously by
the basset and baccarat of the Venetian gaming-
tables; secondly, the invitation to visit Paris
which she received from the great collector and
art-patron, Pierre Crozat; and thirdly, the death,
on 1 April 1719, of her father. His life had been
a hard struggle with scanty means, only softened
towards its close by the fortunate activities of his
clever eldest daughter. But after this last event,
Rosalba, now a woman of five-and-forty, felt herself at liberty to accept Crozat's proposal. Accordingly, in March 1720, she set out for the
French capital with her mother, her two sisters,
and her brother-in-law Pellegrini, who, it should
be stated, had his own special business in Paris.
Returning in 1719 from England, where he had
been working for Lord Cadogan, he had obtained
from John Law, by that date in the plenitude of
his popularity, and whom he had known at Venice,
a commission to paint the ceiling of the gallery of
the recently established Royal Bank. The little

party halted on their way at Lyons. Whether
they came from Avignon by the old crowded 'coche
d'eau,' or drag-boat, is not related; but they eventually accomplished the remainder of their journey
—a matter of five days and some three hundred
miles—in the diligence, which, no doubt, duly
set them down at its terminus, the old fifteenth-
century Hôtel de Sens, near the Ave Maria bar-
racks. Rosalba, her mother, and Giovanna found
lodgment in Crozat's sumptuous mansion in the
rue de Richelieu; Pellegrini and his wife were
accommodated in a neighbouring inn. They
must have arrived towards the end of April; and
in April begins the brief chronicle originally
printed in Italian by the Abbé Giovanni Vianelli,
Canon of Chioggia, and done into French in
1865 by M. Sensier, which is known as Rosalba's
'Journal.' 'Journal' is perhaps too ambitious a
title, since it is often, like the note-books of
Reynolds, little more than a list of sitters and
engagements; but, in both cases, the mere names
are often eloquent.

In 1720 Louis XIV had been dead five years,
and his great-grandson, a boy of ten, ruled in his
stead; that is to say, the reins of government were
in the hands of a Regent, Philip, Duke of Orleans,
to whom his uncle, the Roi-Soleil, had committed

them on his decease. Ever since that occurrence
—or, at all events, during most of the interval—
France had been under the spell of the com-
plicated and specious Mississippi scheme and
'Système,' devised by Law and favoured by
Orleans, for replenishing the exhausted ex-
chequer; regulating the entire revenues of the
kingdom, and exploiting to their full extent the
anticipated resources of the French colonies in
North America. At first a Saturnian age of
prosperity seemed to have set in; huge fortunes
were rapidly made by eager speculators in Mississippi stock; and Law's 'Système' flooded the
country with a profusion of paper-money, ultimately far in excess of any equivalent available
specie. As 'Contrôleur Général des Finances,' the
Scottish adventurer had gone from success to
success, moving his Bank from one vast hotel to
another, loaded with distinctions and landed possessions—the all-powerful idol of the moment.
Nevertheless, in April 1720, the crash was im-
pending. Not many weeks elapsed before the
Government were obliged to issue their first de-
cree reducing the value of the paper currency,
and so to begin the end. By the time Rosalba
got back to Venice, Law had quitted France for
ever, a ruined and discredited man.

But apart from Pellegrini's commission to paint a ceiling at the Bank (which at this precise moment of time must have been in the Hôtel de Mesme, Rue Sainte-Avoie), it was in the nature of things that Rosalba should promptly have entered into communication with her former acquaintance. Her second sitter after her arrival was Law's son, a colourless personage in himself though naturally attracting considerable attention from his paternity. Later on she is painting Law's daughter, Catherine, who after her father's death married her cousin, Lord Wallingford, and, as related in a later paper,[1] became one of the intimates of 'Prior's Peggy,' the Duchess of Portland. At this date Catherine Law was an exceedingly pretty girl, very fresh and unaffected, very French, and universally popular. 'Every one who sought to profit by the "Système,"' says M. Sensier, 'paid court to Mlle Law; Cardinal Bentivoglio, the Pope's nuncio, "jouoit avec elle à la poupée!"' She seems to have been genuinely charming and of irreproachable conduct —recommendations which, nevertheless, did not protect her, in her father's evil days, from the anger of his enemies, as she was injured by a stone-throw at the fair of Bezons. Another early

---

[1] See *post*, 'Prior's "Peggy."'

portrait was that of Rosalba's host's relative, Abbé
Crozat. But her most illustrious sitter was the
boy-King, whom she was privileged first to inspect at Mass in the Church of the Filles Saint-
Thomas, and subsequently, after the fashion of
the day, at breakfast. Finally, she sketches him
for a miniature and also 'en grand.' He must
have been an exemplary sitter, for his Duke-
governor, M. de Villeroi, congratulates her on
his extraordinary patience—a circumstance apparently so remarkable in royalty as to throw
Rosalba's Italian editor, the Abbé Vianelli, into
a transport of sycophancy. But on a later occasion
there was apparently what Captain Costigan calls
a 'conthratong.' 'Three little accidents occurred
to the King,' writes the diarist. 'His gun fell
down, his parrot died, and it went ill with his pet
dog.' Presumably these were accessories in the
picture. But the record would certainly be more
moving were it more precise.

Precision of detail, however, is not one of
Rosalba's characteristics. She frequently shows a
most unfeminine reserve in her chronicle; and it
requires all the aid of M. Sensier's exhaustive
notes to read round her brief memoranda. During the same month of June in which she was
engaged on the portraits already mentioned she

must, by her own account, have seen things
enough to furnish pages of description to a
Walpole or a Fanny Burney. On the 6th, for
example, she notes the beginning at the church
of Saint-Sulpice of the eight-days annual festival
of Corpus Christi, with its imposing procession
of princes and priests (including 'one hundred
young children dressed as angels'), and its chief
'reposoir,' or resting-place for the Host, in the
court of the neighbouring Luxembourg, which
was hung for the occasion with Gobelin tapestries
designed by Raphael, Julio Romano, and Lebrun.
(At this festival it was that the artists of Paris
were accustomed to exhibit their works on the
Pont Neuf, opposite the statue of Henri IV.) She
also visited the famous Galerie du Roi at the
Palais-Royal, and the Académie Royale de Peinture et de Sculpture in the old Louvre, the existing Director of which was the Regent's drawing-
master and painter, M. Antoine Coypel, whose
acquaintance she then made. Another choice
collection she mentions belonged to that accomplished connoisseur and ingenious artist, Philip of
Orleans himself,[1] who had a number of master-
pieces, some of which are to-day in our own

---

[1] 'He had every precious gift but that of making good
use of them,' said his mother, the Princess Palatine.

National Gallery. At the Barefooted Augustins or 'Petits Pères' (where the celebrated musician Baptiste Lulli lay buried), Rosalba saw also many excellent canvases, which her brother-in-law increased by one of his own composition. And naturally she went with him to the newly founded Bank and inspected his design ('modèle') for the adornment of the Mississippi gallery, of which sprawling medley of mythological deities and allegorical personifications M. Sensier prints a long contemporary description. Whether Pellegrini was ever paid for this rapidly-executed performance is still doubtful.

In all probability he was *not*, for the star of the 'Contrôleur Général des Finances' was rapidly declining. In the following July, owing to further depreciation of the new currency, both his coach and coachman were stoned by the exasperated populace; an occurrence which the President de Mesme, who witnessed it, is said to have announced dramatically to the Regent and Council in a tragic impromptu:

> Messieurs, je vous apporte une grande nouvelle,
> Le carrosse de Law est réduit en cannelle.[1]

These things at first only seemed to amuse

---

[1] *I.e.*, 'broken to bits.'

Philip of Orleans, but the Duc de Bourbon, who
had profited scandalously by Mississippi speculations, thought it prudent for a time to carry
Mme. Law and her children out of harm's way
to his domain of Saint-Maur. As for Rosalba,
her diary for this month is unfortunately missing,
and her comments, if any, are not forthcoming.
In August, however, she is engaged on fresh portraits of Crozat and the King; she visits the
famous Medici Gallery of Paintings by Rubens
in the Luxembourg (now in the Louvre); witnesses at Charenton one of those reviews which,
with the boy-regiment known as the 'Royal-
terrasse,' were intended to familiarize the young
king with military operations; and explores the
Versailles of Louis XIV, then abandoned by
royalty for Paris. Another place to which she
went was Trianon; that is to say, the Grand
Trianon of Louis XIV, the Little Trianon of
Louis XVI and Marie Antoinette being a later
enterprise. On the 15th she saw at Saint-Roch
the famous 'procession du pain,' the 'pains'—
apparently of unusual size—being carried as re-
liquaries, and surrounded by candles. This cere-
monial, says M. Sensier, had its origin in an
incident in the life of the patron saint. Attacked
in Italy by the plague, to avoid communicating

that disorder to others, he retired to a solitude. Thereupon, the story goes, bread was brought to him mysteriously by a dog, and he recovered. But perhaps the most interesting entry for August is the curt 'Saw M. Vateau, and an Englishman.'[1] The famous painter of the 'Embarquement pour Cythère' was—as appears from a letter printed by Vianelli—already a warm admirer of Rosalba. Feeble of body and failing in health, he had at this date not long to live, for he died in August 1721. 'Il a fini ses jours le pinceau à la main,' wrote Crozat, for whom Rosalba, in the preceding February, had by request painted a portrait of him, now no longer to be traced.

Commissions multiply in September and October, and Rosalba is kept busily employed. Some of these were from the English Mississippians who swarmed in the French capital, but her most illustrious visitor from this country was the wife of the second Duke of Richmond, who sat to her in October. 'Milady carried away the portrait without . . .' records the diarist, and M. Sensier fills up the blank with the word 'paying,' which, for the credit of perfidious Albion, one trusts is incorrect. In September Rosalba had begun the

[1] Watteau visited this country in 1720.

portrait of Law referred to at the beginning of this paper, but it was not completed until the following November. Notwithstanding these things, she still finds time to attend another review at Charenton; to frequent the Comédie Française and the Opera; and to visit St. Cloud, the Invalides, and the great annual Foire Saint-Laurent, then held in and near the street of that name. Two of her entries reveal her in a new capacity. On 30 September Crozat gives a splendid concert, at which the Regent, Law, the Comte de Caylus, Watteau, and others were present. One of Crozat's objects in this entertainment was to exhibit Rosalba's proficiency as a violinist; and at the Louvre there is said to be a drawing by Watteau, which once belonged to Mariette, giving portraits of the chief performers, Rosalba included. The other event, which took place on 26 October, was the receipt, at M. Coypel's, of a letter announcing that she had been unanimously elected a Member of the Academy of Painting and Sculpture, an honour in those days very rarely conferred upon women. She was admitted on the strength of her portrait of the King; but her diploma work was not sent in from Venice until October 1721. In her covering letter she describes it: 'I have tried to depict a young girl,

knowing that to youth many faults are forgiven.
She also stands for a nymph of Apollo's choir,
who goes, on her own part, to offer to the Academy of Paris a wreath of laurels, judging that
body alone worthy to wear it and to preside over
all the others.'[1]   The picture is still in the
Louvre, where it may be compared with the
pastels of the artist's contemporaries, Joseph
Vivien and Maurice-Quentin de La Tour.

'Bad day,' begins the record for November. 'I
saw M. Law at the bank, and talked to him.'
On the 1st of this month Law's bank-notes
ceased to be current, giving rise to a not unreasonable dissatisfaction, followed by rioting and
tumult.   Matters were not mended by the disap-
pearance—accompanied by considerable funds—
of Vernezobe, one of the cashiers. 'From this
moment,' says M. Sensier, 'the financier who
was to make of France the Eldorado of Europe,
descended, from fall to fall, into the abyss in
which he was to disappear.' How far this 'dé-
gringolade' affected Rosalba she does not say;
but it is significant that, already in October, the
Duc de Villeroi had postponed paying for the
King's picture until payment could be made, not
only adequately, but in coin of the realm instead

[1] Letter to Antoine Coypel, 10 October 1721.

of Law's bank bills. A laconic 'Diminution of
the currency' at the close of November is, however, her only reference to Law and his now
exploded 'system.' Meanwhile, in addition to
completing Law's portrait, she paints Mme. de
Louvois, Mme. de Parabère, and the Duchesse de
Brissac; and she is received at the Academy
with acclamation. She visits Marly, and sees the
grand artificial cascade called the 'montagne de
neige" which tumbled precipitately over some
sixty-three marble steps, and, a few years later,
became too costly to keep up. Whether she also
saw that other stock sight of Marly, the lumber-
ing machine of the Chevalier de Ville for pump-
ing water to Versailles, the portentous groanings
and throbbings of which could be heard miles
away, we know not; but she certainly saw the
'grandes eaux' at the latter place on the same
day, finishing, incongruously enough, with the
hearing of a sermon at the Versailles parish church
from one of the missionaries of the Convent of
St. Lazare. On the 22nd Crozat gives another
concert at which an internuncio performs on the
archilute or theorbo; and three days later the
Regent and his suite visit Rosalba's studio and
watch her at her work.

For December the most interesting entries

curtly record the collapse and flight of Law. He
retired first to Guermandes, near Lagny, one of
his fourteen country seats, whence on the 16th
(provided with a safe-conduct from the Regent)
he escaped to Brussels. Here shortly afterwards
he was joined by his wife who, during his popularity, says Walpole, had lived 'in the most
stately manner' in France. At Brussels he was
received with enthusiasm; and he had the
effrontery to assert that he had enriched the
French nobility and left Paris flourishing. It may
be that the first part of this statement was true;
the second was manifestly false.[1] His day was
done; and as far as Rosalba is concerned he fades
out of the picture. Although he eventually died
at Venice (where he is buried), and she must
have seen him there, their relations appear never
to have been renewed.[2] For the rest, Rosalba's

[1] 'The Regent alone remained true to his ordinary
character, tolerant and mild; issuing with clean hands
from this immense gaming-house (*tripot*).' So says M. Sensier; and it is pleasant to have something favourable to
record of Philip of Orleans.

[2] She was more fortunate than Pellegrini, for she was
paid for her work. 'I received 10 louis of 45 francs for
the portrait of M. Law,' says an entry in the 'Journal' for
21 January. The picture probably went with Law to
England in 1721-5, and thus came on the market.

chronicle of December is increasingly absorbed
by details of sittings and portraits. Beyond a visit
to the manufactory of Gobelin tapestry, which
she inspects in all its branches, the only entry of
interest refers to her presence at the famous ball,
or 'ballet du Roi,' which took place on the 30th
in the 'Salle des Machines' at the Tuileries.
The ostensible centre-piece was a three-act
comedy in prose entitled 'Les Folies de Cardenio'
(Don Quixote's Cardenio) by Charles Coypel,
later a popular illustrator of Cervantes. But more
important than the play were the prologue and
interludes, the dances for which were designed
by Balon, ballet-master to the Court, and the
airs composed by Lalande, the superintendent of
the King's Music. In these the boy-King appeared 'en Amour,' with a suite of dukes, whose
ages ranged from ten to twenty-two, in guise of
'Cupidons'; and we are told that he danced two
'entrées' entirely alone. 'Hymen' (the Duc de
Chartres) and 'Minerva' (Mlle. Antier of the
Opera) figured in other sets; and there were
quadrilles of Spaniards, Moors, Indians, Chinese-
pagods, shepherds, and sailors in which the men
were 'grands seigneurs,' the women being recruited from the Opera. 'I saw the whole Court
in gala,' writes Rosalba: 'it was as magnificent

as it is possible to imagine it.' There were subsequent repetitions, for one of which she was again favoured with tickets. Then the King got overheated by his saltatory exertions and his Governor, the Duc de Villeroi, put a peremptory stop to the performances.

At the close of December 1720 Rosalba had been more than eight months in Paris, and must have been thinking of returning to Italy. She was evidently embarrassed by the number of her commissions, and apparently not a little perturbed by the pressure put upon her to execute certain unpalatable portraits. The Regent she seems never to have painted; but 'I was obliged,' she says, 'to promise to make a portrait of the Archbishop of Cambrai' (the latest and most inappropriate distinction of the notorious Abbé Dubois). Among her visitors of January was Lady Lansdowne, wife of Pope's patron 'Granville the polite,' then an exile in France for the Jacobite tendencies which had led to his imprisonment in the Tower. But at this point we must abridge our extracts from Rosalba's record, which henceforth grows more professional and less general.[1]

[1] A casual anecdote—fitter, perhaps, for a footnote than the severity of a full-wigged page—may be preserved. The Captain of the Gardes du Corps, the Duc de Noailles,

Two of the most important entries chronicle the fact that one of the King's Treasurers, M. Grain, brought her three thousand francs in silver, presumably for the King's portrait, and that, as already stated, she painted Watteau for Crozat. Then, in March, Crozat departed with his nephew for Holland in connection with the Law business; and Rosalba, whose respect for ' les convenances ' seems to have been exceedingly sensitive, prepared to leave the sumptuous apartments she had so long occupied at her host's mansion in the rue de Richelieu. The last entry in the ' Journal ' is dated 11 March. A few days later she set out for her Italian home by way of Strassburg—a route which, after the plague broke out at Marseilles in June 1720, had become popular with travellers. She stopped at Füssen in Swabia, entering Italy by the Tyrol and reaching Venice at the beginning of May. ' Never shall I forget either Paris or Versailles,' she wrote later to

had, in common with some other illustrious persons, a rooted antipathy to cats. The young King, who, on the contrary, was fond of animals, and must moreover have been as mischievous as Tony Lumpkin, tested this one day by pinching him unawares, and ' miaulling.' The poor Duke fainted on the spot, fell heavily to the ground, and hurt himself badly—a disastrous demonstration for which his repentant royal master had the grace to shed tears.

Mariette; but, in spite of many solicitations, she did not again visit France.

She nevertheless continued, in the intervals of her busy life, to correspond regularly with her faithful admirers, Crozat and Mariette. In 1723 she went with Giovanna to Modena to paint the six daughters of the reigning duke. Here, in the ducal gallery, she was fascinated by Correggio's 'Magdalen,' of which she made a pastel copy, subsequently bought by Algarotti for the King of Poland. Returning home, she seems to have been overwhelmed by commissions from all parts of the Continent; and many of her works found their way to this country. 'The English lords keep me busily employed making portraits in pastel,' she writes in 1727 to Mariette. One of her firmest friends was the English Consul at Venice, Joseph Smith, a famous collector of books and pictures. Dilettante Mr. Walpole sneers at Smith's 'title-page knowledge' of his literary treasures; but the man who was responsible for the reproduction of the 1527 edition of Boccaccio's 'Decameron,' and whose books were good enough to be bought by George III for the King's Library in the British Museum, must have been something more than a mere 'Tom Folio.' It is possible that Smith exaggerated the merits of his

Venetian contemporary, Sebastian Ricci;[1] but to the 'merchant of Venice,' as Walpole calls him, is due the fact that many of Rosalba's works came to this country; and one of her most attractive portraits of herself is that she presented to him, which he caused to be engraved by Joseph Wagner.

At Venice in 1725 it was evidently the hour of pastel; and Rosalba, as its most popular exponent, must have found considerable difficulty in complying with the demands made upon her both to teach and practise an art which was in such general request. Everybody was learning it, if not as a business, at least as an accomplishment, or endeavouring to improve it in one way or another. Many of her pupils were, of course, the merest amateurs, but she was largely aided by some who had real gifts. One of these was

[1] 'Do you remember how angry he [Smith] was when showing us a Guido, after pompous rooms full of Sebastian Riccis, which he had a mind to establish for capital pictures, you told him he had now made amends for all the rubbish he had showed us before?' (Walpole to Mann, 18 June 1744). He was surely justly angry, if Mann be quoted textually. Ricci, like his pupil Pellegrini, was long resident in England, and painted altar-pieces at Chelsea College and Bulstrode (see *post*, 'Prior's "Peggy"'), the latter of which included his own portrait.

Felicita Sartori, a humble girl of genius, who afterwards, as Madame Hoffmann, became much sought after in Germany. Another was the poet and dramatist, Luisa Bergalli. Attracted by the vogue of the reigning method, she became Rosalba's pupil, and with Felicita Sartori and Giovanna helped to satisfy the ceaseless demands of visitors to Venice for their portraits in coloured chalks.

In March 1730 Rosalba was summoned to Vienna by the Emperor of Germany, Charles VI, and in October of that year returned to Venice, having painted the Emperor, Empress and Archduchess, with a fair number of the nobility. The Empress,[1] indeed, did her the honour to take lessons from her—'a distinction which,' says Mariette drily, 'one puts willingly into an artist's life although, rated at its just value, it may not mean very much.' The Viennese episode is,

---

[1] Elizabeth-Christine of Wolfenbüttell-Blankenburg was not the only Imperial personage who dallied with pastels. There are said to be several specimens in this kind by Frederick the Great, done when he was imprisoned at Küstrin by his tyrannical father. One of them represents a young woman, and has for epigraph the words, presumably by the artist himself:

> 'Si je pourrois vous complaire;
> C'est là tout ce que j'espere.'

nevertheless, regarded by Rosalba's biographer as
the acme of her career; and for some years to
come her life is little more than an unvarying
round of successful labour, diversified by the music
and song of pleasure-loving Venice, and the facile
and fulsome sonneteering so dear to the Italians.
Rosalba herself was, as we have seen, a capable
musician, playing both the violin and the harpsichord; she sang with taste and feeling, and she
composed airs for the poems that were written in
her honour. Her verse apparently was not her
strong point; and she owned herself excelled,
not only by Luisa Bergalli, who was a professional, but by her sister Giovanna. Thus five
years passed away in a tranquil and unchronicled
uniformity, broken at length by Giovanna's death.
' C'étoit la plus excellente fille du monde,' wrote
Mariette, ' qui étoit la meilleure amie de la
Rosalba, et qu'elle n'a jamais oubliée.' Giovanna
died on 9 May 1737. In the next year followed
the patient and laborious mother, always an essen-
tial figure in the household, who, if she had not
equalled her daughters' gifts, had at least afforded
them a model of diligence and assiduity.

By this date Rosalba was well over sixty. She
was still passionately attached to her profession;
and but for untoward circumstances would doubt-

less have continued to practise it to the end of her life, dying, like Watteau, brush in hand. But she had already begun to be threatened by that terrible affliction—for the artist in particular—the failure of her sight. Owing to this, she had for years abandoned miniature, only executing in 1727, at the express solicitation of Mariette, a solitary portrait for that eccentric amateur and biographer of Watteau, the Comte de Caylus.[1] It was not, however, until 1746 that she recognized unmistakably that the ineluctable hour had arrived when she must no longer continue to work. Her last effort was a picture for her faithful friend Mariette, and it reached him in August 1746. At this date she had laid aside her palette

[1] Anne-Claude-Philippe de Tubières de Grimoard de Pestels de Lévis, Comte de Caylus (the long-drawn sonority of the affixes is irresistible!) had been one of Rosalba's Paris acquaintances, who had interested himself to obtain payment for Pellegrini. He was an amateur and connoisseur of the first water, a friend of all the contemporary artists, living poorly simply to increase, from an ample fortune, the vast collection he left to the King. He died in 1765, being buried in a favourite Egyptian sarcophagus, which was transported to St.-Germain l'Auxerrois for the purpose. For this Diderot wrote the epitaph:

'Cy gist un antiquaire acariâtre et brusque;
Ah qu'il repose bien dans cette cruche étrusque.

for ever. She had cataract in both eyes. In
August 1749 she underwent an operation which
seemed to promise partial recovery, and she wrote
joyfully to Mariette of the future. But her hopes
were not realized, and in the next year she was
completely blind. 'I am totally deprived of sight,'
she tells Mariette in a farewell letter. With her
widowed sister Angela she continued to live in
her little house in the Dorso-Duro quarter, near
the square of San Vito, interesting herself in
such literature of the day as was read to her, and
dictating her correspondence. She was naturally
an object of curiosity to those familiar with her
former reputation; but she shrank from parading
the spectacle of her infirmity and of the melancholy which deepened with decrepitude. All her
life she had been subject to fits of depression, and
these were intensified by her blindness. She made
her last will and testament in December 1756,
leaving the fortune she had acquired by her in-
dustry, some 19,000 ducats (or what in these
days would amount to 240,000 francs), to her surviving sister and her relatives. Four months later,
on 15 April 1757, she died, in her eighty-second
year, and was buried by the side of Giovanna
in the Church of San Vito and San Modesto
in Venice. Angela Pellegrini must have soon

followed her to the grave, for she too was over eighty in 1757.

There are several portraits of Rosalba, the majority by herself. The most authentic is in the Gallery of Painters at Florence, to which she presented it; and she is shown holding in her hand a sketch of Giovanna. Marco Pitteri engraved this portrait, but it is not held to be as attractive as that engraved by Wagner for Joseph Smith. Rosalba's social charm was great; but that she was beautiful can scarcely be contended, though one must be an emperor like Charles VI to dare to say—as he said to Bertani—that she was very ugly ('Ma ella e molto brutta'). In Wagner's engraving (the original picture, if it exists, is not now traceable) she has large, penetrating eyes and a mouth, nose, and chin in which her biographer professes to discover indications of those qualities of intelligence, elevation, tenacity of purpose, and latent humour with which he credits her. Notwithstanding all his efforts, he failed to find any trace of a lover. Rosalba had no romance! She was simply a clear-headed, hard-working, home-keeping craftswoman, devoted to her calling and her family, and reaping deservedly the reward of her prolonged and praiseworthy labours.

ROSALBA CARRIERA

(BY HERSELF, AS ENGRAVED BY WAGNER)

Her works are scattered in many places—in the palaces and Academy of Venice; in her birthplace, Chioggia; at Paris and at Dresden. In the Louvre is her diploma picture; in the Dresden Gallery, her copy of Correggio's 'Magdalen,' with her portraits of Metastasio and the Empress Elizabeth.[1] Many of her productions have, no doubt, perished; but there must still be a considerable number lying 'perdus' in private houses. If she had not the faultless draughtsmanship of La Tour or the minute finish of Liotard, she had an unquestioned freshness and charm of her own. She has left, it is true, no piece of the persistent and ubiquitous popularity (in its engraved form) of Liotard's 'Belle Chocolatière' (Mlle. Baldauf). But pastel was as much born for Rosalba as 'Don Quixote' was born for Cervantes. She cultivated it successfully; she did her best to develop it; and she is fairly entitled to the praise accorded her of adapting to a volatile age the powdery (and perishable) hues of the butterfly.

[1] There is a crayon portrait by her of Henry Stuart, Cardinal York, second son of the 'Old Pretender,' in the National Portrait Gallery; and there are also several specimens of her skill in the National Gallery at Dublin.

STREATHAM PLACE

READERS of those famous 'Roundabout Papers' now regarded as the matured expression of Thackeray's literary idiosyncrasy, may possibly remember that in one of them the author gives an account of two essays he had planned but never written. The first was designed to deal with the mysterious shooting affray between Major Murray and the money-lender in Northumberland Street, Strand, which, in 1861, struck terror to a public already overstrained by the nightly 'sensation headers' of Mr. Dion Boucicault (Myles-of-the-Ponies) in his popular Adelphi drama of the 'Colleen Bawn.' On reconsideration, this idea was rejected as 'too glum and serious' for the semi-playful treatment demanded. The other, handled in the manner of 'Gulliver's Travels,' would have found its pretext in the then-recent adventures of Mons. Paul Du Chaillu in Gorilla-land. 'It was to have contained' (and particular attention is directed to the 'nice derangement' of the wording) 'all the deep pathos of Addison, the logical precision of Rabelais, the childlike playfulness of Swift; the

32

manly stoicism of Sterne, the metaphysical depth
of Goldsmith; the blushing modesty of Fielding;
the epigrammatic terseness of Sir Walter Scott;
the uproarious humour of Sam Richardson; and
the gay simplicity of Sam Johnson.' It must be
admitted also that the scenario supplied is exceedingly attractive. But it so fell out that before
the piece had taken its elaborated form in type,
its author was himself burlesqued by the photo-
graphers as 'A Literary Gorilla,' and to narrate
this particular form of fable became obviously out
of the question.

According to Lady Ritchie's introduction to the
'Roundabout Papers,' these were not the only
things her father had jotted down as likely themes
for what he called his 'pavement sermons.' In
his diaries for 1861-2 she found, as a suggestion,
'On Burning Old Books,' a salutary but sacri-
legious operation, which still occupies the con-
troversialist. Another was to have been 'On
Bread and Butter'—also a burning question; a
third, 'On Titles (magazines, novels, etc.)';
while a fourth might have been prompted by the
obituary notice, carefully transcribed from the
'European Magazine' for 1815, of Martha Gunn,
the famous old Brighton bathing-woman who
the legend ran, had been privileged to 'dip' the

D

youthful Prince of Wales (George IV).[1] But the
memorandum which, for the moment, most at-
tracts us, is for a dissertation on 'Streatham. Mrs.
Thrale. Thrale. Johnson, &c.' Here, it might
be imagined, was a congenial subject. One of
the volumes Thackeray most fondly cherished—
almost as fondly as his bedside ' Montaigne '—was
a cheap and battered old double-column ' Boswell '; and in his works he had only dealt casually
with Johnson. Of necessity Johnson is not included in the ' English Humourists '; and he is
but historically mentioned in the 'Four Georges.'
In the ' Luck of Barry Lyndon,' he is shown
discussing ' a rhyme for Aristotle ' with its un-
worshipful hero, whom Goldsmith has introduced
to him at Button's Coffee-house; while he figures
fitfully (and not always sympathetically) in the
pages of ' The Virginians,' ' a big, awkward,
pock-marked, snuff-coloured man '—now lumber-
ing heavily along Fleet Street; now gulping endless cups of tea at Mrs. Brown's tart-shop in Tunbridge Wells; now tendering the unanswerable

---

[1] There is contemporary caricature and ballad authority
for this; but Mr. Lewis Melville (' Brighton,' 1909, p. 128)
rightly points out that George IV does not seem to have
been at Brighton in his childhood. His first visit was on
the 7th of September 1783, when he was of age.

criticism of slumber to George Warrington's reading of the tragedy of 'Carpezan.' But the picture of him by the author of 'Esmond' in the Southwark brewer's country home, where for some 'twenty years of a life radically wretched' he was at his best and easiest; and where his 'dictes and gestes' were scrupulously chronicled by two such clever observers as Hester Thrale and Frances Burney—is a loss to literature not easily repaired.[1] If we are rash enough to attempt the venture here, it is assuredly from no spirit of emulation, or even of imitation.

In the eighteenth century, the dispersed district now called Streatham was represented by a straggling village, remarkable chiefly for the heathy open spaces[2] in its vicinity, and for the valuable cathartic properties of the water which its medicinal spring supplied freely to the hospitals of the metropolis. Streatham Place, known familiarly to the 'Brighthelmston Flying Machine' as

[1] In 1861 Abraham Hayward published the second edition of his 'Autobiography, Letters and Literary Remains of Mrs. Piozzi (Thrale),' one object of which was to traverse Lord Macaulay's version of the Johnson-Piozzi controversy. Thackeray knew both Hayward and Macaulay; and for this reason, perhaps, never wrote the paper.

[2] Not entirely free from 'squires of the pad,' to whose 'habits of depredation' Johnson refers as late as 1783.

'Thrale's,' and still existent when Thackeray wrote, would probably have been roughly described by its inmates as lying on the right hand of the high road to Croydon, some six miles from Westminster Bridge. To-day, when it has completely disappeared, its site may be more precisely defined as occupied by 'Streatham Park,' a network of short roads and villas lying to the south of Tooting Bec Common. It was a large white, three-storied house, with a projecting centre and wings, standing in a well-timbered enclosure of about a hundred acres, with its 'cattle, poultry, dogs, all running freely about, without annoying each other.' Of the interior we know little. But we hear incidentally of a music-room where Dr. Burney gave lessons on the harpsichord to 'Queenie' Thrale; of a cheerful library adorned with portraits by Reynolds, which was sometimes used to breakfast in; of an adjoining study into which it opened; of a bright saloon hung with sky-blue, gaily-bordered, and of a dining-parlour where Hogarth and other prints were 'pasted on the walls.' Outside, in the spacious grounds, were stables, and a paddock, and high-walled kitchen-gardens, with pineries and ice-houses; and round the whole—as at Stowe—ran a gravelled path—of nearly two miles in extent.

STREATHAM PALACE, SURREY

(FROM A DRAWING BY W. ELLIS, ENGRAVED BY HIMSELF)

There was a lake, or spring-pond, with an island, to which—perhaps in imitation of the ' Duck Island' in St. James's Park whereof Mr. de St. Evremond was the first Governor—its proprietor and contriver had given the name of ' Dick's Island.' This, we learn, was planted with laurels that Johnson watered. We also hear of a walk called after him; of a laboratory where he conducted hazardous chemical experiments; and of a court upon the low entrance-gate to which he leaned, and swung, and read Fontenelle's Memoirs. Last, but not least, there was a 'sweet cool summer-house' where one could write in comfort or—like Miss Burney—study the soothing pages of ' Irene.' In days when the environs of London were less charged with that oppressive atmosphere which broods round an overgrown city, Streatham Place must have been one of the most delightful of rural retirements—a veritable Sans-Souci, with the added advantage of ' sans-gêne.'

Its owner at this date was a wealthy young brewer, Henry Thrale, whose town house was in Deadman's Place (now Park Street) in the Borough, next the Old Anchor Brewery.[1] This

[1] The Old Anchor Brewery, if not actually on the site of the Globe Theatre, must have been in close proximity to it (' Autobiography,' etc., ii, 33).

had come to him from his father, Ralph Thrale, under whom, as manager for an uncle, Edmund Halsey (whose daughter married Lord Cobham of Stowe), the business had prospered prodigiously. Ralph Thrale had become M.P. for Southwark; had married his daughters to persons of condition, and had educated his only son at Eton and Oxford. In October 1763, being then thirty-five, Henry Thrale married Miss Hester Lynch Salusbury, thirteen years his junior, a very clever, if somewhat strong-minded young Welshwoman of good family, with a fortune of £10,000. Miss Salusbury's father, an erratic and irascible parent, had disapproved the match, which was promoted by her mother. In December 1762, however, Mr. Salusbury died suddenly of apoplexy; and ten months later, she was precipitately married to Mr. Thrale by her mother and her uncle, Sir Thomas Salusbury, a widower, who was himself in a hurry to marry a widow: 'My uncle went himself with me to church, gave me away, dined with us at Streatham Park, returned to Hertford-fordshire [Offley Place, near Hitchin], wedded the widow, and then scarce ever saw or wrote to either of us; leaving me to conciliate as I could a husband who was indeed much kinder than I counted on, to a *plain girl*, who had not one attraction in his eyes, and on whom he never had thrown five minutes of his time away, in any interview unwitnessed by company, even till after our wedding day was done!'[1]

A bride with brains and a fortune certainly deserved a better fate, though the result of this hasty alliance was not so disastrous as might have been expected. Miss Salusbury, however 'plain' in her own estimation, was certainly not personally unattractive; and she was, moreover, an exceptionally lively, witty, and for those days, singularly learned young lady. Besides being proficient in French, Spanish, and Italian, she had been carefully instructed in Latin, logic and rhetoric by a preceptor four times her age, Dr. Arthur Collier,[2] with whom her relations must have somewhat resembled those of Charlotte Brontë and M. Heger. 'A friendship more tender, or more unpolluted by interest or by vanity, never existed'—she tells us. 'Love had no place at all in the connection, nor had he [Collier] any rival

---

[1] 'Autobiography,' etc., 2nd ed., ii, 22.

[2] Arthur Collier, D.C.L., of Doctors' Commons. He died 23 May 1777 ('G. M.' for that year, p. 248). He was the son of Arthur Collier the metaphysician (d. 1732), and brother of the Margaret Collier who accompanied the Fieldings to Lisbon. Another of his pupils was Miss Streatfield (see *post*, p. 54).

but my *mother.*' Dr. Collier's influence lasted
until she married, after which we hear no more
of him. With her husband her accomplishments
went for little; though, as a fox-hunter with a
pack at Croydon, he should have appreciated her
excellence as a horse-woman. Tail, dignified
and of good address, but taciturn, slow, and un-
demonstrative, Mr. Thrale had unfortunately, in
addition to a liberal education, enjoyed a too
liberal allowance in his youth, which had converted him into a phlegmatic man of pleasure,
with a fair prospect of becoming, as he eventually
became, a confirmed *bon-vivant.*

His wife was at first a mere chattel, kept in
seclusion at Streatham, or inspected periodically
in the Borough by her large, handsome sisters-in-
law. There she learned that her willingness to
reside in Southwark had been the determining
cause of her being selected by her husband as his
helpmeet, his previous lady-loves having declined
to inhabit that unfashionable locality on any
terms whatever. When her first child (afterwards
Lady Keith) was born, she became of rather
more importance. Then ensued what proved to
be the turning point in her life. Thrale was not
averse from company, especially at dinner; and
he was quite intellectual enough to relish good

conversation, and the give-and-take of discussion. Among the rather miscellaneous bachelor friends who still haunted Deadman's Place was the actor and playwright, Arthur Murphy, who, since the days of his 'Gray's Inn Journal,' had been well-known to Johnson. The Thrales were much impressed by Murphy's accounts of the great man's social gifts, and became desirous to make his acquaintance. This Murphy eventually brought about by causing him to be invited to dinner in order to meet Shenstone's protégé, a certain rhyming cobbler named James Wood-house, who was then attracting public attention, and concerning whom Johnson was supposed to have expressed some curiosity. Accordingly, at four o'clock on a Thursday in January 1765, the meeting took place. All Mrs. Thrale re-membered of the day's talk was, that Johnson exhorted the budding versifier, if wishing to be a good writer, or what was more worth, an honest man, to 'give nights and days to the study of Addison'—counsel he afterwards repeated to the world at large in the 'Lives of the Poets.'[1] Murphy had prepared his host for Johnson's pecu-

[1] According to Dr. Maxwell, of Falkland, he really spoke with much contempt of Woodhouse's performances (Hill's 'Boswell,' 1887, ii, 127).

liarities of figure, dress, and behaviour, and the
new associates liked each other so well that on
the following Thursday (the shoemaker being
suppressed) Johnson dined again in the Borough;
and for every successive Thursday during the
winter repeated his visits, gradually becoming, in
Mrs. Thrale's words, 'their constant acquaintance, visitor, companion and friend.' Later on,
he followed them to Brighton, where, opposite
the King's Head [1] in West Street, the Thrales had
a little house; and missing them, wrote 'a letter
expressive of anger,' which has not survived. To
pacify him, Murphy was again invoked; and his
visits to Southwark became more frequent than
ever. When, in 1766, he fell ill, and was confined to his lodgings in Johnson's Court, Thrale
and his wife went to see him; and finding him
miserably distressed in mind, as well as in body,
persuaded him to quit his close habitation for
Streatham Place. Here, staying some three
months, he remained until October, during the
whole of which time he was devotedly nursed by
Mrs. Thrale. 'I undertook the care of his health

---

[1] This was the name given at the Restoration to the
George Inn, where Charles II stayed in 1651, before his
escape to France after the battle of Worcester ('Brighton
Ambulator,' 1818, pp. 12-19).

(she says), and had the happiness of contributing
to its restoration.' No wonder that ever after,
town-lover as he was, he delighted in the 'com-
forts and conveniences' of this haven of peace
and plenty; and though he playfully rallied his
hostess 'for feeding her chickens and starving her
understanding' in the country, he fully recognized
its value as a happy escape from the petty vexa-
tions of his Fleet Street domesticity and the
'scolding-matches' of Mrs. Desmoulins and
'Poll' Carmichael.

From June 1766, then, until October 1782,
Streatham Place was Johnson's summer residence;
and when he did not make the journey in his
host's post-chaise, he must have often occupied a
seat in the coach that started either from the Old
George Inn in the Borough or the Golden Cross
in the Strand. With his friends of the Mitre and
the Turk's Head, his frequent migrations from
Middlesex to Surrey became a by-word. Strahan
complained to Boswell that the Thrales had
absorbed him; and Goldsmith echoes the impeachment in the 'Haunch of Venison,' where
he makes his pinchbeck feastmaster speak of
Burke and the Doctor as guests who

> eternally fail,
> The one with his speeches, the other with Thrale.

And no wonder! In that delightful white house
which was not so far from the roadway but that
one could see the early bird-catchers on Tooting
Common, he must have had almost every luxury
that opulence could extend to an ailing and unusually unwieldy man between sixty and seventy.
He had obviously his own attendant, for it is on
record that his black servant Francis Barber
married one of Mrs. Thrale's maids. There was,
besides, a watchful valet always ready to bustle
after and intercept him at the parlour door when
he neglected to change his second best wig before
he went to dinner; and as he mounted bedward,
the same inflexible attendant followed him with
another. His chief apartment was the roomy
library, for which he had selected many of the
books, and in which he received his friends and
casual visitors, with full licence to entertain them
if he thought fit. It was in the library that the
proofs of the ' Lives of the Poets' were read aloud
at breakfast by Mrs. Thrale as they arrived from
Nichols the printer; it was in the library that he
'spoke Ramblers' to an attentive audience. When
he ' planned a life of greater diligence,' he retired
to the summer-house, of which Clarkson Stanfield
made a picture in Murray's ' Johnsoniana,' and
indulged his inclination as long as the fit lasted.

As for the commissariat, it was unimpeachable—
as it naturally would be in the house of the
'Amphitryon où l'on dine'; and it must have
more than satisfied the standard of the man who
told Burke he had reached that critical age when
nature 'requires the repairs of a table.' His
'crosses,' moreover, can scarcely have been graver
than the 'smoky chimney' of the too-wealthy
pietest of whom Wesley writes in his 'Diary.'
If Mrs. Thrale's mother, Mrs. Salusbury, who
must have been as inveterate a newsmonger as
Addison's upholsterer, sometimes wearied him by
her incessant inquiries as to 'What the *Swede*
intend, and what the *French*,' he could at least
(and he apparently did) revenge himself by con-
cocting bogus paragraphs about fresh partitions
of Poland, intended specially for her delectation
and mystification. She seems to have been the
only person with whom he got on indifferently
at Streatham Place; and it is pleasant and characteristic to think that as she became infirm and
hopelessly broken in health, he softened and grew
kind. Thrale he seems to have really respected.
He had certainly a higher opinion of his host's
character and abilities than has survived; and he
mourned his death with genuine sorrow. 'I am
afraid of thinking what I have lost,' he wrote.

'I never had such a friend before.' At this time
he had read the will, and can scarcely be accused
of that 'dash of interest to keep his fondness
warm,' which has been attributed to him.[1]

Arthur Murphy, who, as will be remembered,
had introduced the Thrales to Johnson, subsequently wrote an 'Essay on the Life and
Genius' of the latter which compares favourably
with his earlier and more perfunctory attempt on
behalf of Fielding. It was prepared to take the
place of the discursive official account prefixed by
Hawkins to the 1787 edition of Johnson's works.
Murphy was manifestly well acquainted with
both parties; and it might reasonably have been
expected that he would have enlarged upon the
amenities and diversions of Streatham Place. But
beyond stating that Johnson's headquarters were
from 1766 fixed at Streatham; that an apartment
was perpetually reserved for him there; that the
library was enlarged on his account; and that

---

[1] He wrote eulogistic epitaphs on Thrale and Mrs. Salusbury in Streatham Church. It was while at service there
in 1777—says Steevens—that he received his first application from the unfortunate Dr. Dodd. But, apart from his
confessed irregularities as a churchgoer, he could not have
been a very constant attendant at St. Leonard's, as he
generally quitted Streatham for the week-end to preside
over the Sunday dinner of his Fleet Street 'menagerie.'

parties were constantly invited from town to
meet him—beyond these generalities Murphy
attempts no account of the Streatham circle.
Boswell, who did not make Mrs. Thrale's acquaintance until later, is far more vivid and particular; and he is the first to give any adequate
idea of Johnson's position in his new environment, and of the nature of his relations with his
entertainers. His initial visit was in October
1769, when he found his illustrious friend in
'every circumstance that can make society
pleasing.' 'Though quite at home,' he was yet
'looked up to with an awe, tempered by affection,
and seemed to be equally the care of his host and
hostess. I rejoiced at seeing him so happy.'
After a preliminary salvo of sarcasms against the
Scotch, which the compliant Boswell calls 'good-
humoured,' but which must have been most embarrassing in the presence of a new-made friend,
the conversation turned to literature: 'Mrs.
Thrale disputed with him on the merit of Prior.
He attacked him powerfully; said he wrote of
love like a man who had never felt it; his love
verses were college verses; and he repeated the
song " Alexis shunn'd his fellow swains," etc., in
so ludicrous a manner, as to make us all wonder
how anyone could have been pleased with such

fantastical stuff. Mrs. Thrale stood to her guns
with great courage, in defence of amorous ditties,
which Johnson despised, till he at last silenced
her by saying, " My dear Lady, talk no more of
this. Nonsense can only be defended by nonsense." " [1]

The conversation then shifted to Perdita's song
in the 'pastoral drama' adapted by Garrick from
'The Winter's Tale.' Mrs. Thrale praised
(though she slightly misquoted) the line ' They
smile with the simple, and feed with the poor.'
Johnson, who, for the sake of argument, could be
as literal as Monsieur Jourdain, at once objected
against this. It would never do. ' Poor David!
Smile with the simple; What folly is that? And
who would feed with the poor that can help it?'
No, no, for his part let him smile with the wise,
and feed with the rich. Boswell was busybody
enough to repeat this to Garrick, and wonders
that Garrick was annoyed. He tried to console
the ruffled Roscius by comparing Johnson to

[1] Hill's 'Boswell,' 1887, ii, 78. He took the same
ground in the 'Lives of the Poets' (Hill's ed. 1905, ii,
202): 'In his [Prior's] " Amorous Effusions " he is less
happy; for they are not dictated by nature or by passion,
and have neither gallantry nor tenderness.' But—with
every deference to the critic—*all* Prior's love-songs are
not on the model of ' The Despairing Shepherd.'

Horace's pushing ox, with the hay on its horns.
' Ay (said Garrick vehemently), he has a whole
mow of it.' Mrs. Thrale's not unnatural comment
on this is: ' How odd to go and tell the man!'

The accounts by Boswell of his visits to Streatham Place are, however, scanty and unimportant.
In 1778, when he went ' by the coach,' he records a desultory conversation in which Johnson
is made to utter words of wisdom on the topic of
truth-telling in narration, the oblique motive of
which appears to have been to enable Boswell to
deplore the deviations from exact authenticity
of his predecessors, Sir John Hawkins and Mrs.
Thrale. On another occasion he relates the ill-
success of his first endeavours to secure the assistance of Pope's executor, Lord Marchmont, for
Johnson's life of Pope, then in progress. Johnson,
it is evident, either resented Boswell's officious
intervention, or shrank from incurring an obligation of which the utility might be doubtful.
However, a year later, when he came expressly
from Streatham to see Lord Marchmont, he was
'exceedingly courteous,' and told Boswell (who
of course accompanied him) that he would rather
have given twenty pounds than not have come—
an admission which, nevertheless, did not prevent
him from neglecting to make use of his hench-

E

man's notes of the interview. Boswell seems frequently to have dined in the Borough, if he did
not often do so at Streatham Place. And in the
Borough, as at Streatham, it certainly 'snewéd of
mete and drynke.' The Thrale table was, in fact,
a tradition. Writing later of a grand feast at
'The Ship' at Brighton, Miss Burney speaks of
it as 'nothing to a Streatham dinner'; and in
these ascetic days, when we are assured by the
Faculty that only the most moderate of menus
can possibly 'keep us out of Harley Street,' the
brewer's bill of fare suggests nothing so much as
the heterogeneous banquet in Swift's 'Polite
Conversation.' Johnson (as Garrick might well
have retorted!) had excellent reasons for preferring
to 'feed with the rich.'

Besides being casual, Boswell's Streatham memories are always coloured by his jealousy of the
clever woman whose vivacious 'Anecdotes' had
anticipated his own more ambitious 'Life.' But
with August 1778 he was succeeded by a chronicler whose record—at all events at first—was entirely rose-coloured. From Fanny Burney's
'Diary' of her visits to the Thrales in that, and
the following year, we get a far more intimate
picture of the life there than can be obtained
elsewhere. To the successful young author of

the just published 'Evelina,' everything was delightful; and every wind blew her praises in her eyes. Dr. Johnson, who, at her father's house, some seventeen months before, had appeared to her in the light of an extraordinarily uncouth and unmannerly eccentric [1] was now—although she was still conscious of his 'cruel infirmities'— transformed into a benevolent and beatific patron. He took a fancy to her at once; paid her elaborate compliments, direct and indirect; and was unwearied in his commendation of her novel. 'Richardson,' he declared, 'would have been

---

[1] Here are some sentences from her first impressions written to her mentor, Mr. Crisp, a few days after the event: 'He [Doctor Johnson] is, indeed, very ill-favoured; is tall and stout; but stoops terribly; he is almost bent double. . . . He has a strange method of frequently twirling his fingers, and twisting his hands. His body is in constant agitation, *see-sawing* up and down; his feet are never a moment quiet; and, in short, his whole person is in *perpetual motion*. His dress, too, considering the times, and that he had meant to put on his *best becomes*, being engaged to dine in a large company, was as much out of the common road as his figure; he had a large wig, snuff-coloured coat, and gold buttons, but no ruffles to his shirt. . . .' ('Early Diary,' 1907, ii, p. 153). The passages indicated as omitted appear to have been subsequently softened or modified, for which reason they are not reproduced here.

really afraid of her; there is merit in 'Evelina' which he could not have borne. No; it would not have done! unless, indeed, she would have flattered him prodigiously. Harry Fielding, too, would have been afraid of her; there is nothing so delicately finished in all Harry Fielding's works as in " Evelina." ' To comprehend this hyperbole one has only to recall the equally high-pitched laudation which Fielding bestowed on the 'Arabella' of Mrs. Charlotte Lenox. These great men (Fielding and Johnson) were not ashamed of commending what pleased them; and they rejoiced in the 'noble pleasure of praising.' But with all allowances for the over-emphasis of partiality, there can be no doubt that the Doctor showed his best side to his new friend. Dr. Goldsmith, he said, was his last hero; he had had none till his 'little Burney' came.

Yes: at Streatham Place he was decidedly 'en belle humeur': and although the almost ferocious frankness of his dislikes and the equally energetic candour of his goodwill were frequently out of all proportion to the occasion, it must have been delightful (when you were uninvolved) to listen to his caustic comments on Wilkes and Garrick, his anecdotes of Boyse and Savage, his 'boutades' at Mrs. Montagu and Sir John Hawkins, his

chaff of the colourless Mr. Crutchley and the inoffensive Sir Philip Jennings Clerke. And if it
was vexatious to find your costume dissected by
a critic who, blind of one eye and scarcely able to
distinguish colours with the other, had yet an un-
canny knack of discovering anything wrong, it
was surely impossible to resist his grave enjoy-
ment of the fantastic vagaries of the anomalous
Bet Flint, or his solemn speculations on the de-
sirability of making the unprecedented addition of
a roasting-jack to the 'batterie de cuisine' at Bolt
Court. That he must have been often distress-
ingly mute and uncommunicative ('the ghost
that never speaks until it is spoken to'—and
sometimes not even then!) is undeniable; it is
clear also that, particularly when he was ill, he
was not seldom inexcusably rude and over-bear-
ing. But you never could tell when the latent
spring of tenderness would be unsealed; and his
sudden kindnesses had all the restorative consola-
tion of a burst of sunlight in bad weather. 'I am
always sorry when I make bitter speeches (he
told Mrs. Thrale), and I never do it but when I
am insufferably vexed.' And then he would assure
her that she had borne his scolding like an angel;
or that she never talked nonsense; or that she had
as much sense and more wit than any woman he

knew—things which made her wish (quoting Miss Burney) 'to go under the table.' As regards Miss Burney, he said to her face: 'I admire her for her observation, for her good sense, for her humour, for her discernment, for her manner of expressing them, and for all her writing talents.' After that, talk of ' approbation from Sir Hubert Stanley! '

Many visitors who deserve more notice than those who have been already mentioned came and went at Streatham Place during the Johnson-Thrale period. But it is not always bishops such as their Graces of London and Peterborough, or aristocrats such as Col. Holroyd and Lord Mulgrave, or great ladies such as Mrs. Crewe and Mrs. Boscawen—who fall easiest under the pen of the describer. One of Fanny Burney's most finished portraits is that of the prude-coquette, Miss Sophy Streatfield of Tunbridge Wells, whose gift of shedding tears at will, lent so much fascination to the lackadaisical charms which subjugated her host; another is that of Mr. Seward, the author of ' Biographiana,' and as blasé as Sir Charles Coldstream in ' Used Up.' But the lions of the Streatham circle were fortunately perpetuated by the brush of Reynolds, thirteen of whose works decorated the library. From the Burney

'Diary,' we can almost recover their exact positions. Mrs. Thrale, and 'Queenie' (the eldest
daughter), at full length, hung over the fireplace.
This was the largest picture. Mr. Thrale himself

> —from intruders defending his door,
> While he wishes his house would with people run o'er,

surmounted the entrance to his 'study,' an apartment which, in regard to its equipment, one
always fancies must have resembled that of Major
Ponto in the 'Book of Snobs.' This is, however,
a possible injustice, for he had done decently at
Oxford. The remaining portraits, three-quarters
like Mr. Thrale's, were ranged above the book-
cases. They comprised Thrale's early friends,
Lord Sandys and Lyttelton's brother, Lord West-
cote, Johnson, Burke, Goldsmith, Murphy, Garrick, Baretti, Sir Robert Chambers and Reynolds
himself. Dr. Burney, one of the last executed,
ends the list. Mrs. Thrale, as might be expected,
did not like her own portrait. There was 'really
no resemblance,' she said, 'and the *character* is
less like *my* father's daughter than Pharaoh's.'
The same view appears in the rhymed description
she wrote of it:

> In these features, so placid, so cool, so serene,
> What trace of the wit or the Welshwoman's seen?

What trace of the tender, the rough, the refin'd,
The soul in which such contrarieties join'd?
Where, tho' merriment loves over method to rule,
Religion resides, and the virtues keep school;
Till when tir'd we condemn her dogmatical air,
Like a rocket she rises, and leaves us to stare.

She wrote similar verses for all the gallery—of very varying merit and admittedly dashed with satire. To her firm ally, Murphy, she is too kind; to Goldsmith and Burke unsympathetic. She was not hard enough on the cross-grained and vindictive Baretti. Of the conversation of Reynolds, she writes:

Nothing in it o'erflows, nothing ever is wanting,
It nor chills like his kindness, nor glows like his painting.
When Johnson by strength overpowers the mind,
When Montagu dazzles, and Burke strikes us blind,
To Reynolds well pleas'd for relief we must run,
Rejoice in his shadow, and shrink from the sun.

Garrick is conventionally treated. Last comes Johnson:

Gigantic in knowledge, in virtue, in strength,
With Johnson our company closes at length:
So the Greeks from the cavern of Polypheme past,
When, wisest and greatest, Ulysses came last.
To his comrades contemptuous, we see him look down,
On their wit and their worth with a general frown:

While from Science' proud tree the rich fruit he receives,
Who could shake the whole trunk, while they turned a
    few leaves.
Th' inflammable temper, the positive tongue,
Too conscious of right for endurance of wrong,
We suffer from Johnson, contented to find
That some notice we gain from so noble a mind;
And pardon our hurts, since so many have found
The balm of instruction pour'd into the wound. . . .[1]

In April 1781 Thrale, who had for some time
been in failing health, and whose tastes as a
gourmand had grown morbid, died suddenly of

----

[1] 'Autobiography,' etc., 1861, 2nd ed., ii, 179. The
last six lines, in which Johnson is not very fortunately
compared to 'rectified spirit, sublime alcohol,' are omitted.
The 'Streatham Gallery' was sold in 1816, with the
house—the largest sum realized, £378, being for Johnson's
portrait. Watson Taylor bought this, and it afterwards
formed part of the Peel Collection. Mrs. Thrale and
'Queenie' went eventually for 78 guineas to Mr. S. Bod-
dington, a 'rich merchant,' at whose sale in 1866 they
passed to Louisa, Lady Ashburton, by whom the picture
was exhibited in 1888 at the Grosvenor Gallery, No. 163.
The rouge with which, according to Mangin's 'Piozziana,'
Mrs. Thrale sought to dissemble the ravages caused by a
too early use of cosmetics, was as faithfully reproduced by
Reynolds as by S. P. Roche in her Bath miniature thirty-
six years later; and by its unavoidable contrast with the
youthful freshness of her daughter, then about seventeen,
may unconsciously have added to her distaste for the pic-

apoplexy, brought on by over-eating.[1] His death, with its consequent reduction of his widow's income, materially altered the state of affairs at Streatham. Mrs. Thrale speedily found that the expenses were 'ruining her,' and that it was impossible to go on in the old lavish way on two thousand a year. The situation naturally became strained on both sides. Johnson himself was ill and nearing his end; and with his entire concurrence the house was let to the Prime Minister, Lord Shelburne, for three years. Johnson's leave-taking of the spot so long familiar to him was sad enough. On Sunday, 6 October 1782, he attended service at St. Leonard's for the last time. 'Templo valedixi cum osculo,' he writes. And then he characteristically and methodically sets down in detail and in Latin the items

ture. The portraits of Garrick and Burney were bought in 1816 by Dr. Charles Burney, of Greenwich, and in 1905 were in the possession of the late Archdeacon Burney, of Surbiton. ('Diary,' etc., of Mme. d'Arblay, 1905, vi, p. 297.)

[1] Lest this should seem too severe, let the unwilling witness, Johnson, speak. Two days before Thrale's death he felt constrained to say to him at dinner: 'Sir, after the denunciation of your physicians this morning, such eating is little better than suicide.' ('Autobiography,' etc., 1861, 2nd ed., i, 132.)

of his last dinner: 'Roast leg of lamb with spinach chopped fine, the stuffing of flour with raisins, a sirloin of beef, and a turkey poult; and after the first course figs, grapes not very ripe owing to the bad season, with peaches—hard ones. I took my place in no joyful mood, and dined moderately that I might not at the lest fall into the sin of intemperance.' On the following day, having early 'packed up his bundles,' he made his 'parting use of the library.' 'I read St. Paul's farewell in the Acts, and then read fortuitously in the Gospels.' [1]

'Streathamiam quando revisam?' had been the closing words of his Sunday entry. He was never to see it again when he set out on the morrow to join Mrs. Thrale at Brighton. He was then ill, for he notes that he had to rest 'four times in walking between the inn and the lodging.' And he was eventually to have a greater grief in the later loss of that friendly and enlivening intercourse which had meant so much to his easily dejected and gloomy nature. Already, in 1780, Mrs. Thrale, during her husband's lifetime, and on Fanny Burney's introduction, had made the acquaintance of Gabriel Piozzi, an Italian mu-

[1] Birkbeck Hill's 'Johnsonian Miscellanies,' 1897, i, 109.

sician, 'with gentle, pleasing, unaffected manners,' and of unblemished character. As time
went on they became mutually attached. Before
1782 matters had gone so far that she had determined to marry him. Her daughters—to
whom their father had left £20,000 each—were
opposed to the match, as indeed were many of
her friends; and in January 1783, after a struggle,
she bade him farewell. But it was beyond her
powers; her health began to suffer; and Piozzi
was recalled from Milan. Finally, on 23 July
1784, with the tacit consent of her children, she
married him according to the rites of the Roman
Catholic Church, to which he belonged. A
second marriage took place on the 25th at St.
James's, Bath. Johnson, as might be expected,
regarded the whole affair as 'ignominious.' He
expostulated in terms which she describes as
'unmerited severity,' and she defended herself
and her future husband with much dignity and
spirit. Johnson's rejoinder, in a more temperate
tone, contained the familiar recognition of 'that
kindness which soothed twenty years of a life
radically wretched.' To this she returned 'a
very kind and affectionate farewell.' When she
left for Italy she was in truth too happy to care
much for opinion public or private. Her first

marriage had been ' arranged '; her second was
of affection, and she never repented it. Piozzi
managed her affairs with admirable skill and
economy, and she nursed him in his last days
with the utmost devotion. After his death, in
March 1809, she wore mourning for the rest of
her life.

As the title imports, this paper has been more
occupied with Mrs. Thrale's house than with
Mrs. Thrale. Those who desire further information respecting this gifted and remarkable woman
will have to seek it in the oft-quoted volumes of
Abraham Hayward and in the additional material
contained in Mr. A. M. Broadley's interesting
' Dr. Johnson and Mrs. Thrale,' which has the
advantage of a learned ' Essay Introductory ' by
Mr. Thomas Seccombe. A pleasant little pamphlet entitled ' Streatham Old and New,' by
H. B[aldwin] n.d., may also be consulted. In
regard to Streatham Place, however, it is needful
to add that, on returning to England, the Piozzis
inhabited it from 1790 to 1795. They endeavoured at the outset to reconstruct the old
hospitable life; but, in spite of coloured lamps
and covers for seventy people, the attempt did
not succeed. The conditions were changed, and
the cost beyond their means. They moved to a

villa ' in the Italian style,' which Piozzi built on
his wife's property near Denbigh. When he died,
Streatham Place, which by this date had become
Streatham Park, seems to have been a white
elephant to his widow. In November 1814,
when her tenant was Count Lieven, she speaks
of having new-fronted the house, and new-fenced
the hundred acres at a cost of £6,500. In 1816,
as already related, she sold it, books, pictures,
and all. Its last owner was a Mr. Phillips, by
whom, in 1863, it was pulled down. There is a
Thrale Road still on the old site; and, in 1832,
Thrale Almshouses were erected by Lady Keith
and her sisters.

FALCONER'S 'SHIPWRECK'

IN some of those fluent pages of Fanny
Burney's 'Diary' which relate how her func-
tions as Queen Charlotte's Dresser brought her
in due time to Cheltenham to drink the waters
with King George III, there is passing reference
to Falconer's now forgotten poem. Among the
members of the depleted Court which accompanied His Majesty was the Queen's Vice-
Chamberlain, Colonel Stephen Digby, whose
identity in the 'Diary' is discreetly veiled as
'Colonel Fairly.' At this date he was a widower
of five-and-forty with four children, and still
sufficiently under the influence of bereavement to
be sentimentally interesting. In the confined
premises and undress atmosphere of Lord Faucon-
berg's borrowed house at Bay's Hill, there were
exceptional facilities for the intimate study of
character; and between 'Colonel Fairly' and
Miss Burney—as all the world knows—there
ensued what, if it did not precisely amount to a
definitive affair of the heart, was at least a decorous exchange of preliminaries. They drank

63

tea *tête à tête*; discussed theology and minor ethics
in 'a genteel roundabout way'; and together
perused the poets of the period. Among the
earlier works which 'Colonel Fairly' read with
the author of 'Evelina' was 'The Shipwreck,' a
masterpiece of which, although it was then a
quarter of a century old, the lady, strangely
enough, had never heard. It was 'somewhat too
long,' 'Colonel Fairly' thought; it was also
'somewhat too technical'; but 'it contained many
beautiful passages'—a not unfair summary, being
indeed pretty much the general verdict the poem
would probably receive to-day in any modern
manual of English literature that condescended
to notice it. Some of its 'beautiful passages' the
Colonel read aloud to Miss Burney while she
worked, extolling, in particular, the masterly
portraits of the officers (so unlike the seamen of
Smollett!), lingering over the pathetic love-story
of Palemon (a name surely never borne on any
Georgian ship's books!), and sighing deeply at
the 'sweet line':

He felt the chastity of silent woe—

an evidence of sensibility which his listener, looking to her companion's own forlornly viduous
condition, could not fail to regard as 'extremely

affecting.' The readings were resumed with increased interest; and from Falconer the students passed to Akenside and 'The Pleasures of Imagination '—where we may leave them, since our immediate purpose is to pause at the author of 'The Shipwreck.'

The facts of William Falconer's life are few and indefinite; and the Rev. James Stanier Clarke, Domestic Chaplain and Librarian to the Prince of Wales (afterwards George IV), and Vicar of Preston,[1] who put forth a sumptuous edition of 'The Shipwreck' in 1804, showed considerable ingenuity in stretching his slender material into a 'biographical Memoir' of thirty-four pages. In this place we need not follow his example. Falconer's father was, like Allan Ramsay,

---

[1] Clarke himself had been a seaman; and in this respect, although he cannot claim to rank as a superlative literary critic, should have been a competent editor of Falconer. He was later the author of a laborious life of Nelson, of which the merit is marred by its garbled correspondence. Perhaps the most memorable thing about him is his fatuous suggestion to Miss Austen, after she had dedicated 'Emma' to the Prince Regent, that she should, apropos of the approaching marriage of the Princess Charlotte and Prince Leopold, try her hand at 'an historical romance illustrative of the august house of Cobourg'—a counsel she was wise enough to neglect.

F

an Edinburgh barber and wig-maker. He carried on a precarious calling in an old-fashioned,
wooden-fronted shop at the Netherbow Port,
near John Knox's Corner; and either for his
son's sake, or his own, is credited with natural
ability and much humour. Falconer was born in
February 1732;[1] and according to his own account, received from one Webster, no more than
an elementary education in 'the three R.'s.' But
as he lived to compile an elaborate 'Marine
Dictionary,' and is later affirmed to have been
'never at a loss to understand either French,
Spanish, Italian, or even German,' he must, as
time went on, have contrived to extend his
acquirements. He did not follow his father's
trade; but 'reluctantly'—as appears from his
later utterances—served his apprenticeship on
board a Leith merchant vessel. His next reported employment was that of servant to the
purser of a man-of-war, such purser being none
other than the Archibald Campbell who afterwards coarsely and clumsily satirized Johnson as

[1] This is the date given by Carruthers and the 'Dictionary of National Biography.' But Mitford says 'about
1736 or 1737, which would make Falconer between
fourteen and fifteen when in 1751 he published his first
poem on the death of Frederick, Prince of Wales.

'Lexiphanes'; and who, if we may believe Sir
John Hawkins, 'as well for the malignancy of
his heart as his terrific countenance, was called
horrible Campbell.'[1] However this may be,
Campbell, according to another authority, the
Dr. James Currie who edited Burns, delighted
in giving instruction to his subordinate; and
when Falconer afterwards obtained celebrity,
boasted of the success of his scholar—a course
which scarcely bears out the words of Hawkins.
The author of 'Lexiphanes' is not a congenial
personage; but it must be remembered that
Hawkins himself has been described as incor-
rigibly censorious.

The good offices of Campbell are supposed to
have procured for Falconer his next post, that of
second mate to a vessel in the Levant trade, which
shortly afterwards was shipwrecked on the coast
of Greece, three only of the crew surviving, of
whom Falconer was one. This was the catastrophe which prompted the later poem of 'The
Shipwreck,' although by how much it preceded
the appearance of that work is not known, the
exact date of the occurrence having never been
ascertained. But the circumstances must naturally have been vividly impressed on Falconer's

[1] 'Life of Samuel Johnson,' 1787, 2nd ed., p. 347.

memory, and the connection of ' The Shipwreck '
with its author's personal experience is manifest,
seeing that the ' Britannia ' of the poem, a mer-
chantman proceeding from Alexandria to Venice,
and touching at Crete, suffers total loss near Cape
Colonna (the ' Sunium's marbled steep' of Byron,
and the ' Sunium's height' of Landor), the crew,
except three, being drowned.

' The Shipwreck,' however, was not published
until May 1762; and all we know of the
author in the interim is that he probably remained
in the merchant service. But for at least ten
years previously he must have practised verse-
writing. His first printed metrical production
was a formal ode on the death, in March 1751,
of Frederick, Prince of Wales, a performance
which is neither better nor worse than the many
celebrations of that not-immoderately deplored
event; but, having regard to its writer's ante-
cedents, whether written at fourteen or nineteen,
it is certainly remarkable. One of its couplets,
in which the poet invites Melpomene to enable
him

> To assist the pouring rains with brimful eyes,
> And aid hoarse-howling Boreas with my sighs,

recalls the hyperbole of Dryden, or, better,
Dorset's

But let him know it is our tears
Bring floods of grief to Whitehall stairs.

where the rhyme is nearly as bad as the figure.
Falconer is subsequently supposed to have ' re-
lieved and strengthened his mind' by contributing
a few poems to the pages of Sylvanus Urban, but
they do not bear his signature. The first, which
purports to have been written by 'J. W., a
Sailor,' has for subject the 'uncommon scarcity
of Poets in the " Gentleman's Magazine " for
December last,' and does nothing particular to
repair the deficiency it deplores; another, in May
1759, a ' Description of a Ninety Gun Ship,' is
certainly in Falconer's later manner:

But leaving feignèd ornaments, behold!
Eight hundred youths of heart and sinew bold,
Mount up her shrouds, or to her tops ascend.
Some haul her braces, some her foresail bend;
Full ninety brazen guns her port-holes fill,
Ready with nitrous magazines to kill,
From dread embrazures formidably peep,
And seem to threaten ruin to the deep;
On pivots fix'd, the well-rang'd swivels lie,
Or to point downward, or to brave the sky;
While peteraroes swell with infant rage,
Prepar'd, though small, with fury to engage,
Thus arm'd, may Britain long her state maintain,
And with triumphant navies rule the main.

To which last couplet we may devoutly answer
'Amen!' 'Colonel Fairly' would perhaps have
called these lines already too technical. But, as
Victor Hugo says, 'Quand la chose est, dites le
mot'; and it is surely better to speak plainly of
'hauling braces' and 'bending foresails' than to
transfigure the 'poop-lantern' into 'a Pharos of
distinguished blaze,' as Falconer does in an
earlier line.

Clarke appears to have wished to identify
Falconer with the composition of the popular sea-
song known as 'The Storm'; or, more familiarly,
'Cease rude Boreas,' an interminable eight-verse
ditty of eight-line stanzas, with which that fine
tenor and quondam-mariner, Benjamin Charles
Incledon, not only contrived to hold his hearers
at Ranelagh and Vauxhall, but even to rouse
them to a furore of enthusiasm. The only other
person likely to have written the song, in Clarke's
opinion, was captain Edward Thompson, the
editor of Marvell, and the author of many popular sea-songs. But Chappell long ago disposed of
Falconer's authorship on chronological grounds;[1]
and words and tune are now definitely assigned
to a third clever song-writer, the George Alexander Stevens whose grotesque 'Lecture on

[1] 'Popular Music of the Olden Time,' ii, 786.

Heads' used, in Foote's day, to delight the fre-
quenters of the little Theatre in the Haymarket.
A second poem, or fragment of a poem, attributed
to Falconer both by Chalmers and Mitford, but
printed by neither, deserves, if only for its local
colouring, more attention than it has hitherto
received. It is not unlikely that it belongs to the
time when Falconer himself was numbered with
the class of which it professes to depict the habitat
afloat. It is entitled ' The Midshipman,' whose
quarters at this date were on the orlop, or lowest
deck, in close proximity to that region where,
' Pills in his rear, and CULLEN in his front,' the
Ship's Surgeon, or 'lop-lolly man,'[1] assisted by
his mates (not all of them potential Goldsmiths
or Chattertons), aligned his gallipots and dressed
the wounds of war. Hard by, the ' Mid.' is shown
making obstructed toilet in order to dine ' in
high Olympus' with the Officers; anon grum-
bling, after his wont, with his fellows over Mess-
Debts, Discipline, and Slow Promotion; finally

[1] Readers of Mrs. Piozzi's 'Anecdotes' may recall how
Dr. Johnson's verbal delicacy was outraged by this rude
sea-term. In 1762 he asked an officer of the ' Belleisle '
what some part of that man-of-war was called; and was
told it was ' where the lop-lolly man kept his lop-lolly '—
a reply which he regarded as ' disrespectful, gross, and
ignorant.'

dividing his attention between preparing a dish
of Lobscourse or Lobscouse ('Lapscous,' Falconer calls it), and puzzling his brains with the
sines and tangents which are to help him—if the
good fates please—to a Sub-Lieutenant's commission:

> Now to the Longitude's vast height he soars,
> And now formation of LAPSCOUS explores;
> Now o'er a field of Logarithms bends,
> And now, to make a Pudding he pretends:
> At once the Sage, the Hero, and the Cook,
> He wields the Sword, the Saucepan, and the Book.
> Oppos'd to him a sprightly Mess-mate lolls,
> Declaims with GARRICK, or with SHUTER drolls;
> Sometimes his breast great CATO's virtue warms,
> And then his task the gay LOTHARIO charms;
> CLEONE's [1] grief his tragic feelings wake,
> With RICHARD's pangs th' ORLOPIAN CAVERN shake!
> No more the Mess for other joys repine,
> When Pea-Soup entering shows 'tis time to dine.
>   But think not meanly of this humble Seat;
> Whence sprung the Guardians of the BRITISH FLEET:
> Revere the Sacred Spot, however low,
> Which formed to Martial acts—an HAWKE! an HOWE!

By one of Falconer's earlier biographers it was
asserted that Falconer entered the navy before
1760, and was shipwrecked for a second time in

---

[1] This helps to fix the date, for 'Cleone' was first
played on 2nd December 1758.

Byng's old flagship, the 'Ramillies,' which was
lost in the Channel in February 1760, with all
hands, except 'one midshipman and twenty-five
men.'[1] This, however, has since been conclu-
sively contradicted by the publication of his log,
showing he was elsewhere. But it is quite possible that the loss of the 'Ramillies' stimulated
him to give metrical form to his still vivid
memories of the 'Britannia' catastrophe. In any
case '"The Shipwreck." A Poem. In Three
Cantos. By a Sailor, price 5s.,' was duly 'printed
for the Author' and published by Andrew Millar
in the Strand in May 1762. It was in the cus-
tomary quarto form; and the dedication to the
King's brother, His Royal Highness Edward,
Duke of York, who had then hoisted his Flag
as Rear-Admiral of the Blue on the 'Princess
Amelia,' was signed 'William Falconer.' It
'succeeded,' says Clarke, 'from the moment it
appeared,' and even the saturnine review of
Griffiths, in which Kenrick had followed Goldsmith, was not only laudatory but extravagant.
The author was freely compared to Homer—
not to Homer's advantage. 'Homer,' said the
'Monthly Review' (xxvii (1763), pp. 198, 200),
'has been admired, by some, for reducing a

---

[1] 'Gentleman s Magazine,' 1760, p. 100.

catalogue of ships into tolerably flowing verse;
but who, except a poetical Sailor, the nursling of
Apollo, educated by Neptune, would ever have
thought of versifying his own sea-language? what
other Poet would ever have dreamt of reef-tackles,
hall-yards, clue-garnets, bunt-lines, lashings,
lannyards, and fifty other terms equally obnoxious
to the soft sing-song of modern Poetasters.' They
are certainly—to use the words of a gifted critic
recently taken from us [1]—'kittle to scan.' But
the reviewer does not stint his praise, for he goes
on to say that many of Falconer's 'descriptions
are in our opinion, not at all inferior to anything of the kind we meet with in the Æneid;
many passages in the third and fifth books of
which, we conceive nevertheless our Author has
had in view. They have not suffered, however,
by his imitation; and his Pilot appears to much
greater advantage than the Palinurus of Virgil.' [2]
Falconer, in short, in this critic's eyes, is such a
'Virgilius Nauticus' as should have delighted the
M. Bergeret of the 'Mannequin d'Osier.'

Passing from these contemporary fireworks,
which, at all events, exhibit a praiseworthy disposition to welcome novelty of theme and execu-

[1] Andrew Lang, *ob. eheu!* 20 July 1912.
[2] 'Monthly Review,' September 1762, p. 197.

tion, we may linger for a moment on ' The Shipwreck' in its earliest published form, which is, of
course, that examined above. There is always a
prepossession in favour of the first 'sprightly running'; and despite some illustrious adventures
in extension, it is not unintelligible. Falconer
made numerous additions, alterations, and trans-
positions in his second and third issues; and the
text of the poem, as he finally revised it, differs
materially from the text originally put forth by
Andrew Millar, which is now before us.[1] It is
arranged in three cantos, the first of which, after
due invocation of the Muses, deals with the sail-
ing of the 'Britannia' from Candia in Crete.
There are signs of storm at the outset, which increase as the ship proceeds along the northern
coast of the island; and by the time Cape
Malacha has been left astern and Cape Spada
sighted, she has to reef her topsails. Thereupon
the first canto closes. It contains a good deal of
historical and descriptive padding; but this, as

[1] By the courtesy of Mr. Edmund Gosse. This now
rare impression, it may be added, is preceded by a careful
chart of the ship's path from the port of Candia to Cape
Colonna; and also by an elaborate 'Elevation of a Merchant Ship with all her Masts, Yards, Sails and Rigging.
Both of these are said to be designed by Falconer himself.

Byron said, is not the author's strong point. His
strong point is the ship and her doings. They
pass a shoal of dolphins, heralds of bad weather,
one of which, entangled in the chains, is har-
pooned:

> Th' upturning points his pond'rous bulk sustain;
> He strives to disengage himself in vain;
> On deck he quivers in extatic Pain:
> Now, as the near approach of Death he feels,
> And flitting life escapes in sanguine rills,
> What radiant changes strike the astonish'd sight!
> What glowing hues of mingled shade and light!

Here, 'secundum artem' (the art of the day),
Phœbus is invoked to parallel the 'varied beauties'
which,

> from his sides, in bright profusion flow,
> That, now in gold empyreal seem to glow,
> Now beam a flaming crimson on the eye,
> And now assume the purple's deeper dye;
> Now in pellucid sapphires strike the view
> And emulate the bright celestial hue.

Off Mount Jove they 'descry'

> A liquid column, tow'ring, shoot on high—

in other words, that sea-whirlwind, a waterspout:

> The fluid vortex in rotation flies,
> Diffusing briny vapours o'er the skies:

This vast phænomenon, whose tow'ring head
In heav'ns immers'd, embracing clouds o'erspread,
In spiral wheels, as Mariners suppose,
First rises, when the raging whirlwind blows.
(The swift volution, and th' enormous train,
Let physical hypotheses explain).
The horrid apparition now draws nigh,
And all around the angry billows fly—

only to be dispersed by a timely broadside from those 'nitrous magazines' of which the vessel in the 'Elevation' displays a formidable row.[1]
In the final version the last line reads:

And white with foam the whirling billows fly.

Both the Dolphin episode and the Waterspout are transferred to the second canto without material alteration, save that 'lofty' takes the place of the repeated word 'tow'ring,' and

Still round, and round, the fluid vortex flies

is substituted for

The fluid vortex in rotation flies.

---

[1] The presence of these guns is worth noting, since, according to Mitford, it had been advanced as confirming Falconer's alleged connection with the loss of the 'Ramillies' man-of-war. But as a matter of fact, and as the 'Elevation' shows plainly, merchantmen trading to the Levant were armed.

Instead of the flat and matter-of-fact

> Let physical hypotheses explain,

Falconer puts:

> Let sages versed in Nature's laws explain.

As to these and other modifications, some more, some less happy, the reader will decide in accordance with his prepossession in favour of first thoughts. With the opening of Canto II the real business of the narrative begins. As Crete is left behind, the sea rises, the sky lowers, and a sudden squall splits the mainsail to ribbons. The vessel veers, hauling again upon the wind; a fresh mainsail is bent; and in the gale the topsails are furled, and the top-gallant-yards sent down. While reefing the mainsail four men are washed off the lee-yard-arm:

> In vain, to grapple pendent ropes they try,
> The pendent ropes a solid gripe deny:
> In vain they cry for aid, with panting breath,
> And faintly struggle with th' approach of Death:
> Th' impetuous surges gath'ring o'er them, sweep,
> And down they sink, forever,[1] to the deep:
> Their sad companions their lost state bemoan;
> Perhaps a fatal prelude to their own.

---

[1] This negatives the contention of Calverley, in 'Fly-Leaves,' that 'our rude forefathers' regarded 'forever' as two words.

By this time, in view of a storm, a high sea, and a lee-shore which the ship cannot hope to weather, the officers are growing apprehensive. They decide to lie broadside to the wind and sea. To this end the mizen is reefed, a procedure which necessitates a hubbub of sea-terms, for which (Captain Cuttle would say) one must 'overhaul' one's 'Sailors' Word-Book':

> Adown the mast, the yard they low'r away,
> Then jears and topping-lift secure belay;
> Soon, o'er the head the circling canvas past,
> Around the yard and sail the gaskett 's fast:
> The reef enwrapp'd, th' inserted nittles ty'd,
> The hallyards, thrott and peek, are next apply'd:
> The order 's given, the yard aloft is sway'd;
> The brails are gone; th' extended sheet belay'd.

After this the crew are suddenly warned by the pilots to 'grasp every man a shroud.' A tremendous sea breaks over the vessel fore and aft, carrying with it the companion, boats, and binnacle, and strewing the deck with compasses and glasses. The strained hull springs a leak, necessitating the manning of the pumps. Then, as the wind increases, the guns are flung overboard; the leak grows apace; and the panting workers are worn out. Meanwhile the ship drives helplessly before the storm, and as she nears the dangerous lee-shore, the skipper warns the crew of this coming peril, and gives them general directions. Finally, the helm becoming useless, and the lowering of the mizen-yard without effect, orders are given to cut away the mizen-mast, which accordingly goes crashing over the quarter, furnishing the canto with a final Virgilian simile, which is a favourable sample of Falconer's manner in this kind. It has besides the advantage of being derived, not, as in other instances, from hackneyed recollections of the ancients, but probably from his own experiences of the hold of a man-of-war:

> Thus, when some limb is seiz'd with gangren'd pains,
> That spread their baneful influence thro' the veins,
> Th' experienc'd Artist all his Skill applies,
> To check the dire contagion as it flies;
> But, if the malady eludes his Art,
> To save the whole, he wisely dooms a part;
> T' impede the Death increasing pangs convey,
> Lops from the trunk th' infected branch away.

With exception of another simile in the orthodox fashion, and a short classical excursus in which the author compares his attempts

> in ornamental verse to dress
> The harshest sounds mechanic Arts express

to the efforts of Orpheus and Dædalus, Canto II, keeps the narrative well in hand. But in the third canto, while the ship, having cleared away her mizen-mast, veers before the wind, a long space is filled with descriptive decoration, in the form of an appeal to Memory. The Argument bristles with capitals. Socrates and Plato, Xerxes and Lycurgus, Ulysses and Penelope, Leander and Hero, Delphos, the Muses, Parnassus, Helicon, are all invoked; and more than two hundred and forty lines have been devoted to these irrelevancies before the poet returns to the 'Britannia,' scudding swiftly under bare poles past the island of Falconera to her inevitable doom. After a terrific night of tempest, darkness, meteors, and thunder and lightning, dawn comes at last, and under the lee rise the hills of Greece. The ship is driven broadside to the shore; her bowsprit, fore-mast, and main-topmast disappear; she strikes a rock, and splits asunder.

> Down, on the vale of Death, with horrid cries,
> The fated Wretches trembling, cast their eyes,
> Lost to all Hope, when lo! a second shock
> Bilges the splitting Vessel on the rock;
> Her groaning bulk the dire concussion feels,
> And with upheaving floods she nods and reels;
> Repeated strokes her crashing ribs divide,
> She loosens, parts and spreads in ruin o'er the tide.

Some of the crew have already been carried away with the main-topmast; others, clinging to the

G

mainmast, reach the rocks only to slip back, ' be-
num'd and feeble,' into the sea; others again,
thrown from the main-yard-arm, are dashed on
the reefs and ' expire without a groan.'

> Four Youths, depending on their Skill in vain,
> On oars and rafts descend into the Main,
> Of whom, by sweeping surges one is drove
> Ashore, all maim'd, a ling'ring Death to prove;
> The rest a speedier end of Mis'ries knew,
> And press'd the stony beach, a lifeless Crew.
> Next from the rigging, terrible to tell!
> Shook from their hold, nine grasping Sailors fell:
> With these the Chief and second in command
> Increas'd the numbers on the death-fraught strand.
> Five grapple yet secure the floating mast,
> Of all the former gallant Crew the last,
> Till two no longer can their grasp retain,
> But sink immers'd and never rise again.
> The rest surviving, whom the surf up-bore,
> Untouching rocks, were haply washed ashore:
> And here they found reclining on the strand,
> The first advent'rous Youth who gained the land;
> Who, when his former Comrades still alive
> He saw, with languid Joy his eyes revive;
> Then, with a feeble groan, resigned his Breath,
> And peaceful sunk into the arms of Death.

After which, with the rescue of the three
survivors by the natives, the poem closes.

That is—closes in its first form, as the poet
conceived it. It has manifest faults: some in-

separable from its period of production; some
arising from literary inexpertness. In the first
canto there is too much 'prolusion,' as Browning
calls it; in the last there are too many classical
references; while in the middle part the nautical
terms are too numerous. But the lines are often
picturesque and vigorous—graphic with the un-
invented presentation of the 'thing seen.' If the
writer could only have forgotten Pope's 'Iliad'
and Dryden's 'Virgil'; if he could have refrained
from interrupting his narrative to remember Zeno
and Epictetus; if he could have confined himself
to the exact description of the scenes which, he
admits, still rose so vividly before his eyes, his
work would have gained appreciably in force and
directness. But so far from seeking to compress,
he expanded, either of his own accord, or 'by
request of friends.' The reader has no doubt remarked that in the poem as quoted above, the
characters of the Master and Officers, and that
history of Palemon which Miss Burney and
'Colonel Fairly' found so touching, are not
mentioned. They are not mentioned because
they are not there. All these and the relative
parts of 'The Shipwreck' were added subsequently; and added—one may suppose—in deference either to some feeling on the writer's part,

or to some suggestion from without, that his work would gain by the addition of further human interest. The portraits of the officers are drawn with considerable skill, and evidently from life. Albert, the master, is the type of the better-class seaman, devoted to the wife and weans he has left at home; beloved by his crew, and thoroughly expert in all the details of his profession. In mid-eighteenth century, and with Smollett's Oakums and Crampleys in mind, the description sounds ideal; but Falconer's editor assures us that the picture is a true one. Rodmond, the first mate, is a rougher specimen. A hardy north-country-man, bred like Cook in that nursery of navigators, the London coal trade, he has gained his know-ledge by experience rather than education. More-over, he had been reared among a lawless com-munity of wreckers:

> Thus RODMOND, trained by this unhallowed crew,
> The sacred social passions never knew.
> Unskill'd to argue, in dispute yet loud,
> Bold without caution, without honours proud:
> In Art unschooled, each veteran rule he prized,
> And all improvement haughtily despised.
> Yet, though full oft to future perils blind,
> With Skill superior glow'd his daring mind
> Through snares of death the reeling Bark to guide
> When midnight shades involve the raging tide.

A third portrait is that of the author himself, under the style of Arion; and it hints indefinitely at some thwarted youthful ambitions;

> Forlorn of heart, and by severe decree
> Condemned reluctant to the faithless Sea,
> With long farewell he left the laurel grove
> Where Science, and the tuneful sisters rove.
> Hither he wandered, anxious to explore
> Antiquities of Nations now no more;
> To penetrate each distant realm unknown,
> And range excursive o'er the untravelled zone.
> In vain—for rude Adversity's command,
> Still on the margin of each famous land,
> With unrelenting ire his steps opposed,
> And every gate of Hope against him closed.

If we are to accept this passage as autobiographical, it would seem, coupled with the further statement that Arion joined the ship at Alexandria, after wandering ' thro' many a scene renown'd,' to imply that Falconer's personal inclinations were rather in the direction of foreign exploration than a seafaring life. But here we are wholly in the region of conjecture. His choice of the name Arion is thus justified:

> For like that Bard unhappy, on his head
> Malignant stars their hostile influence shed.
> Both in lamenting numbers, o'er the deep
> With conscious anguish taught the Harp to weep;

> And both the raging Surge in safety bore
> Amid destruction, panting, to the shore.

How far the account of the fourth personage, Palemon, is founded on fact, it is impossible to say. In the first edition he is simply an unnamed and "advent'rous Youth" who, in the extract quoted on p. 82, reaches land only to die of his injuries. With the enlargement of the poem, he has become an unfortunate lover, whom an opulent and arbitrary parent, the owner of the vessel, has sent abroad in order to separate him effectually from a young lady, Anna, to whom he is devotedly attached, and who is the daughter of the Master, Albert. In the lonely watches Palemon confides to the sympathetic ear of Arion the ' painful secret' of his soul, and at this point comes in ' Colonel Fairly's ' line:

> He felt the chastity of silent woe.

The whole episode is in the taste of the time—a time, it must be remembered, when the epithet 'sentimental' was gradually growing to be one of the hardest-worked words in the language— but the story, as narrative, is by no means ill-told. There seem, however, to have been readers, even in 1764, who thought that the veracious note of the first version lost something by the

later interpolations, justified though those interpolations might be by their vibration of 'la corde
populaire.'

The second edition of 'The Shipwreck' was
not published until 1764, when the first edition
had long been sold off; and in the interval several
things had happened to Falconer. By the advice
of the Duke of York, he had quitted the merchant
service, and entered the Navy, being rated as a
Midshipman on board Hawke's flagship, the
'Royal George.'[1] It must have been at this
period that the already quoted fragment, 'The
Midshipman,' was composed. But two of his
occasional pieces manifestly belong to this date.
One is an ambitious 'Ode on the Duke of York's

---

[1] 'Perhaps,' says Mitford, with unexpected caution,
'the very same ship, the funeral knell of which was so
musically tolled by the Bard of Olney.' There is no need
for 'perhaps.' The 'Royal George' that went down with
Kempenfeldt at Spithead in August 1782, was the same
'Royal George' with which in July 1759 Hawke had
fought Conflans at Quiberon Bay; and was consequently
the same vessel in which, three years later, Falconer wrote
poems to his Royal patron. We have before us a little
inkstand of old sea-stained oak by which the memory of
the author of 'The Shipwreck' is now linked to that of the
two great Admirals. A minute brass plate bears the words
'Model of Capstan from the Wreck of "Royal George"
Sunk 1782 Raised 1839.'

second departure from England as Rear-Admiral,' concerning which we are told specifically that it was composed in the contracted seclusion of a small space between the Ship's side and the cable tiers—the cable tiers being, as we know from 'Roderick Random,' the main haunt of the midshipmen: the other, entitled 'The Fond Lover,' printed in the October number of the 'St. James's Magazine,' where it is dated from the 'Royal George' at sea, 12 August, records, in true Vauxhall fashion, the poetic pangs of the writer's attachment to the daughter of the surgeon of Sheerness Yard, a certain Miss Jane Hicks, whom he afterwards married. According to Mitford, 'The Fond Lover' suggests 'that the fort of Miss Hicks's affection and virtue did not surrender until after a doubtful and protracted siege—' a statement which shows considerable constructive sagacity in the critic, since the lines are of the most conventional kind. Miss Hicks, or 'Miranda,' had also poetical talents, but is said to have made an excellent and devoted wife.

With the cessation of hostilities and the Peace of Paris, the 'Royal George' was paid off. Lack of service-time for a Lieutenant's commission obliged Falconer to resign the military for the civil side of the navy; and in 1763 he was appointed Purser of the 'Glory' frigate. He still, however, continued his literary pursuits, and while the vessel was laid up in ordinary at Chatham, was fortunate enough to attract the attention of Mr. Hanway, a Commissioner of the Navy and brother of Jonas Hanway, the philanthropist. Mr. Hanway was delighted with the genius of the purser of the 'Glory,' and by his friendly offices the Captain's cabin was ' fitted up with a stove, and with every addition of comfort that could be procured; in order that Falconer might thus be enabled to enjoy his favourite propensity, without either molestation or expence '—an act of beneficence which could scarcely have been rivalled by the famous Captain Reece of the 'Mantelpiece.' At this date it must have been that Falconer revised the second edition of 'The Shipwreck,' to which he added several hundred lines. He also tried his hand at a satire, on the Court side, directed mainly against Pitt and Wilkes, as well as Churchill, a reference to whose Gotham

(While fools adore, and vassal bards obey,
Let the great monarch ass through Gotham bray!)

fixes the date at 1764, the year when ' Gotham ' was published, and in the November of which Churchill died. Satire was not Falconer's forte,

and 'The Demagogue,' if sometimes vigorous, is
also sometimes flat and sometimes inflated, while
nothing but the partisan ardour of faction can
defend its abuse of the elder Pitt, whose policy,
pension, and wife's peerage are all noisily denounced.

The most important of Falconer's occupations
at Chatham, however, must have been the com-
pilation of his 'Universal Dictionary of the
Marine.' Probably he had already had this for
some time on the stocks, as in the 'Preface' to
the second edition of 'The Shipwreck,' he refers
to the inadequate works of this kind then in the
market; and he continued to labour at the book
assiduously until, in 1769, it was duly issued
to subscribers as a guinea quarto by Andrew
Millar's successor, Thomas Cadell of the Strand.
The " Dictionary " was a task for which he had
obvious qualifications; and it received the immediate approval both of the naval authorities
and the public. It became a property to its publisher, and went through several editions. Naturally, in these days of steam, electricity, and wire-
less telegraphy, it has become—as Admiral Smyth
says in the 'Preface' to his 'Sailor's Word-Book'
—'imperfect'; but those who desire to understand thoroughly the economy of the men-of-war

commanded by Hawke and Howe, must consult
the 'Marine Dictionary' of Falconer.

In 1767 he was transferred from the 'Glory'
to the 'Swiftsure,' and in the same year died his
patron, the Duke of York. Apparently Falconer
came to London, still working at his 'Dictionary,'
and is said to have been miserably poor; but no
very definite information is forthcoming. He must
nevertheless have been well known as a working
man of letters, for in October 1768 he was invited by an old Edinburgh friend, Mr. John
M'Murray, or Murray, the founder of the now
famous house in Albemarle Street,[1] to join him
as partner in a bookselling enterprise. Mr. Murray
was at this date a second Lieutenant in the
Marines. But he was tired of the inaction which
had followed on the Seven Years' War; and he
was preparing to purchase the business of William
Sandby, opposite St. Dunstan's Church in Fleet
Street. At Chatham he had renewed his former
relations with Falconer. He was to be 'ushered
immediately into public notice' by new editions
of Lord Lyttelton's 'Dialogues of the Dead' and

[1] The present Mr. John Murray's 'Monthly Lists'
still bear a little picture 'of the ship adopted as his emblem
by Lieut. John Murray when he sold his commission and
founded the business in 1768.'

'History of Henry II'—which to-day do not
sound exactly like projects to conjure with.
'Many Blockheads in the Trade,' he wrote, in
concluding his letter, 'are making fortunes; and
did we not succeed as well as they, I think it
must be imputed only to ourselves.' Falconer's
answer to this proposition is not extant; but it
may be assumed that it was in the negative. He
was subsequently appointed purser to the 'Aurora' frigate, Captain Lee, which was proceeding
to India with Messrs. Vansittart, Scrofton, and
Forde, who were charged with the supervision of
the affairs of the East India Company. Falconer
was eventually to be their private secretary. The
rest of the story must be briefly told. The 'Aurora' sailed from Dover on 2 October 1769,
touched at the Cape in December, and was never
heard of again. Whether she was burned at
sea by misadventure, or whether she foundered in
the Mozambique Channel, are still matters of
debate.

A third edition of 'The Shipwreck' was issued
at the end of November 1769. In the Author's
'Advertisement,' dated from 'Somerset House,
October 1' (the day before the 'Aurora' sailed),
it is claimed that the poem had been subjected to
a further 'strict and thorough revision.' In this,

it has been suggested that Falconer received assistance from his compatriot Mallet, who is incidentally mentioned; but Mallet had been dead for
more than four years. Mrs. Falconer contrived
to retain her husband's apartments at Somerset
House, then—as Churchill says sneeringly in the
' Ghost '—' a mere *lodging pen*'; and it is pleasant
to think that the continued sale of ' The Shipwreck ' and the ' Dictionary ' enabled Cadell to
' supply her liberally with money.' She survived
her husband until March 1796, and is buried on
the north side of Weston Church near Bath.
Falconer is described as being what he was most
proud to be called—a Sailor. He was hard-
featured and weather-beaten, blunt of speech and
awkward of address. Although combative in
argument and constitutionally critical, he is said
to have been by nature kindly and generous. His
literary range was limited. He unquestionably
possessed the material to produce, and the capacity
to complete, a poem of exceptional originality,
vigour, and veracity. Probably in any case it
would have been ' too technical.' It was his misfortune that the taste of his time induced him to
encumber a plain tale with conventional ornament, and to pad his pages with manufactured
pathos. He would have done better to rely for

his effects on the inherent horror and misery of the facts. But he lived in days when sentimentalism was rampant; and it was thought poetical to speak of a ship's poop-lantern as 'a Pharos of distinguished blaze.'

PRIOR'S 'PEGGY'

LADY MARGARET CAVENDISH HOLLES HARLEY, otherwise Her Grace the Duchess of Portland, and (for the purposes of this paper) the 'noble, lovely, little Peggy' of Matthew Prior, should certainly not be dismissed as a negligible eighteenth-century figure. Without possessing the triumphant charm of the poet's 'Kitty'—that imperious Katherine Hyde who, as Duchess of Queensberry, vanquished the untamable Swift, and petted and pampered peach-loving John Gay—Margaret Harley remains interesting both by her personality and her environment. From her father and her grandfather she inherited the 'virtuoso whim' which almost from childhood made her a collector of curiosities; she was learned in natural history, botany, and domestic medicine; she was a past-mistress in the manifold 'accomplishments' of her period, including some that even then must have been exceptional; and she succeeded in attracting about her several of the cleverest of her feminine contemporaries. She made an admirable wife to 'the handsomest man in England'; she was an affectionate and judicious mother, and she may justly claim to rank among the more memorable of the 'grandes dames' of the Georgian era. Her letters, and the letters of her correspondents, are an inexhaustible lucky-bag of those detached social details which, trifling in themselves, serve, when brought together, to give congruity and precision to the picture of a time.

She was born in London on 11 February 1715 —her father being Edward, Lord Harley, son of Robert Harley, first Earl of Oxford and Mortimer. Her mother, Henrietta or Harriet Cavendish Holles, was the daughter and heir of the first Duke of Newcastle. At Lord Harley's seat of Wimpole in Cambridgeshire she must have first become known to Prior, who then had not long to live. There, or at Westminster, he saw her frequently, and seems to have been charmed by her infantile attractions. When she is no more than two years old, he sends his 'love—for it is a very pure and innocent passion—to little Margaretta.' His letters to her parents seldom fail to mention her particularly, with every variety of 'dear diminutive,' English and Latin. She is the 'Chara Infantula,' the 'chère ange,' 'little Pearl,' 'her Peggiety,' the 'little incomparable Lady,' his 'dear friend and honoured Peggy.' When he

makes her mother a present of eight pigeons, the
first tribute he has received from his new estate
at Down Hall in Essex, it is coupled with an
express injunction that two of them, 'properly
incrusted with sweetbreads and "sparagrass,"'[1]
shall be roasted immediately 'for his dear little
Lady's private table.'[2] He drinks her health on
all occasions 'de tout son cœur'; and when he,
being, as he says, 'a very laborious poet,' turns
a complimentary couplet to her father in the
library at Wimpole (it is not one of his best),
nothing gratifies him so much as to hear 'little
Mademoiselle Harley' repeat it the next morning 'with the prettiest tone and manner imagin-
able.'[3] Finally he writes her a rhymed epistle:

> My noble, lovely, little PEGGY,
> Let this, my FIRST-EPISTLE, beg ye,
> At dawn of morn, and close of even,
> To lift your heart and hands to heaven:
> In double beauty say your pray'r,
> *Our father* first, then *notre père*;

---

[1] Steele also speaks of ' Chickens and Sparagrass ' in
'Tatler,' No. 150, which shows that the corruption must
have been current. Boswell, too, uses it (Hayward's
'Autobiography, etc. of Mrs. Piozzi' (Thrale) 2nd ed.,
1861, i, 54).

[2] Portland MSS. (Hist. MSS. Comm.), 1899, v, 620.

[3] *Ibid.*, v, 611.

H

And, dearest CHILD, along the day,
In ev'ry thing you do and say,
Obey and please my LORD and LADY,
So GOD shall love, and ANGELS aid, Ye.

If to these PRECEPTS You attend,
No SECOND-LETTER need I send,
And so I rest Your constant Friend,
                              M. P.

This bears date 9 April 1720.[1] In the following year Prior died at Wimpole after a brief illness. He had composed more than one epitaph
' for his own monument'; but perhaps the truest
testimony to his individual charm is the after-
statement of 'Peggy' herself—as reported by
Lady Louisa Stuart—that he was 'beloved by
every living thing in the house—master, child,
and servant, human creature or animal.'[2]

There is a portrait of Margaret Harley about
this date by the popular Swede, Michael Dahl,

---

[1] Bath MSS. (Hist. MSS. Comm.), 1908, iii, 481.
[2] Lady M. Wortley Montagu's 'Works,' by Lord
Wharncliffe, 1837, i, 63. It may here be added that
Mr. Francis Bickley, who contributed a valuable article entitled ' New Facts about Matthew Prior ' to the ' Quarterly
Review' for January 1913, has recently (May 1914) published a life of the poet and diplomatist which leaves
nothing to be desired.

who painted her father. In this she appears as a
quaint, long-waisted, stiff-skirted little personage,
with hair tightly drawn back from an unusually
high forehead. But despite the flat and uninspired
manner of the master, the picture probably repro-
duces, with sufficient fidelity, the child of five celebrated by what Wraxall terms 'Prior's expiring
Muse.' At all events, save a few formal references in Pope's and Swift's correspondence with
her father, it is all we have to rely on until the
date of her marriage some fourteen years later.
Her mother, whom Prior qualifies as 'adoranda,'
seems to have been more worshipful than intellectual. She is also described as exceedingly proud,
and a great stickler for the strictest buckram of
etiquette. With the wits who were her husband's
habitual associates—Prior always excepted—she
got on but ill, and (said her daughter) hated Pope
in particular. Lord Harley, a kind-hearted, in-
dolent, unambitious man, was a confirmed dilet-
tant and connoisseur, to whom belongs the credit
of completing the famous Harleian collection of
MSS., begun by his father, and now in the
British Museum. In the further prosecution of
his 'taste,' he seems also to have contrived to
spend (or squander) on pictures, medals, busts,
and objects of art in general, some £400,000 of

his wife's fortune. This was a side of the paternal character which in a measure reflected itself in the daughter, who, from a very early age, began to gather together shells, feathers, precious stones, and rarities of all sorts. Under Lady Harley and a governess (Miss Walton), she was carefully brought up, and by the time she was twenty must have been what was then regarded as exceptionally well-educated. Being an heiress, she had soon a number of suitors. On the 11th of July 1734 she became the wife of William Bentinck, second Duke and third Earl of Portland; and, according to his father-in-law, one of the most estimable of men. He was the grandson of King William's famous favourite, and at this date was six-and-twenty. The wedding took place at Oxford Chapel (now St. Peter's, Vere Street), which had been built some ten years before from the designs of the James Gibbs to whom we owe Prior's ornate tomb in Westminster Abbey.

Oxford, Cavendish, Harley, Wimpole, Bentinck, and other names connected with the great Portland property thus created, still linger in the region of Marylebone. Indeed, the bulk of the parish which (with its nine medicinal springs) had been bought in 1710 by the first Duke of Newcastle, eventually passed to the Duchess. But the im-

THE DUCHESS OF PORTLAND'S HOUSE AND MUSEUM AT WHITEHALL

(FROM A DRAWING BY J. BROMLEY)

mediate result of her marriage was not only to
invest her with a prominent social position, but
to make her mistress of a convenient house in
town and a great country-seat. The town house
stood in the old Privy-Garden at Whitehall,
occupying the site of the apartments by the
water-side once tenanted by Charles II, and still
easily discernible on Fisher's well-known plan of
the palace.[1] As far back as 1696, the Duke's
grandfather had obtained a building lease of the
ground from William III. Two years later, in
the second fire at Whitehall, the so-called 'Earl
of Portland's lodgings,' with the adjacent Ban-
queting House of Inigo Jones, fortunately escaped
destruction; although both—says a contemporary
record—were 'much damnified';[2] and it must
have been after this catastrophe that the building
so long inhabited by Margaret Harley was constructed or completed.[3] Many years subsequent
to her death, its place was taken by No. 4, Whitehall Gardens, the home of Sir Robert Peel, who,

[1] This, by the way, was dedicated to the second
Duke.

[2] Hope Johnstone Papers (Fifteenth Report of the Hist.
MSS. Comm., App., Pt. ix, 1897, p. 103).

[3] In the Crace Collection at the British Museum is a
view of the House of the late Duchess of Portland in the
Privy Garden, drawn by J. Bromley in 1796.

substituting a new house for the old one, resided here until his fatal accident in 1850, a date, of course, far beyond the limits of this paper. But these apparently gratuitous particulars are justified by the mournful fact that the Whitehall Gardens of to-day, with all its time-honoured memories, must presently be superseded by a range of modern —and probably painfully modern—government offices!

The Duke's country-seat, Bulstrode or Bulstrode Park, in Buckinghamshire, lies to the west of Gerard's Cross, on the left hand of the high road from Uxbridge to Beaconsfield.[1] The house,

---

[1] The Duchess of Portland preferred to spell it Bullstrode, and those who—with Captain Fluellen—decline to 'mock at an ancient tradition,' will excuse if they cannot imitate her. According to Burke's 'Vicissitudes of Families,' the estate, in the days of the 'galloping Normans,' was held by a sturdy Saxon named Shobbington, who, when the Conqueror granted the land to one of his retainers, prepared to dispute the transfer. He and his friends had no horses; but they had a number of bulls. Mounting these improvised chargers, they fell at nightfall on the invader's camp, and put it to flight. After this daring exploit, Shobbington was summoned to Court, a mandate to which he responded riding on a bull, and escorted by seven stalwart sons. In the sequel, he took the oath to William, and was allowed to keep his property. The Duchess, believing devoutly in the 'bull-striders,

erected by a former proprietor, Judge Jeffreys,
has long made room for a later structure. Horace
Walpole, who saw it in 1755, describes it as 'a
melancholy monument of Dutch magnificence,'
having, nevertheless, 'a brave gallery of old pictures, and a chapel with two fine windows of
modern painted glass.' And although in 1762 the
Duchess made him a handsome present of 'portraits of the court of Louis Quatorze' (which
can scarcely have been improved by the fact that
they had been used as targets in the nursery), he
is still ungrateful enough to write of the place in
the following year as 'Dutch and trist.' Mrs.
Lybbe Powys, who inspected it subsequently, is
scarcely as critical as fastidious Mr. Walpole. It
is well worth seeing, she reports; and she praises
the paintings and curiosities, especially 'a Holy
Family as large as life, by Raphael,' and 'The
Building of Antwerp' from Sir Luke Schaub's
collection:

'The hall [she goes on] is surround'd by very
large pieces of every kind of beast by Snyders.[1]

always insisted on writing the name of the place with the
second 'l.'

[1] These were probably the pictures described in Britton
and Brayley as Hunting Scenes by Snyders and his Pupil,
i, p. 393.

The menagerie, I had heard, was the finest in England, but in that I was disappointed, as the spot is by no means calculated to show off the many beautiful birds it contains, of which there were great variety, as a curassoa, goon (?), crown-bird, stork, black and red game, bustards, red-legg'd partridges, silver, gold, pied pheasants, one, what is reckon'd exceedingly curious, the peacock pheasant. The aviary, too, is a most beautiful collection of smaller birds—tumblers, waxbills, yellow and bloom paraquets, Java sparrows, Loretta blue birds, Virginia nightingales, and two widow-birds, or . . . "red-breasted long twit'd finches." Besides all above mention'd, her Grace is exceedingly fond of gardening, is a very learned botanist, and has every English plant in a separate garden by themselves. Upon the whole, I never was more entertain'd than at Bulstrode.'[1]

The date of Mrs. Lybbe Powys' visit to Bulstrode was July 1769, and her description of the 'menagerie' is of necessity an anticipation. But whatever the defects or beauties of the mansion, its environment was magnificent. The pleasure-gardens were held by landscapist judges to be per-

[1] 'Passages from the Diaries of Mrs. Philip Lybbe Powys,' 1899, pp. 120-1.

fect; and the surrounding park of some eight
hundred acres, 'composed of perpetual swells and
slopes, set off by scattered plantations, disposed
in the justest taste,'[1] was one of the most beautiful in England. Fine old trees abounded; and
there were walks which offered effective 'pros-
pects' of Windsor Forest and the blue hills of
Surrey. So various in their expanse were these
extensive grounds as to prompt the story that the
second Duke was once actually stopped in his
own domain by the notorious Dick Turpin—a
pleasant legend which is chronologically possible,
as Turpin was hanged in 1739. Nowadays it
would be easy to get to Gerard's Cross from
Whitehall under an hour; but in 1735 it was
frequently made a leisurely affair, to be broken at
Acton. Yet, on occasion, it could be performed
'à grande vitesse,' as for example in January 1739.
'We set out from Bulstrode at eleven, and were
in town by half an hour over two, over hills of
snow and heaps of ice; but our horses flew as if
each had been a Pegasus—four coaches and six,
with twelve horsemen attending, besides apothe-
caries, bakers, butchers, that joined in the procession to escort us part of the way.' And this
cavalcade could not have included the servants'

---

[1] 'Ambulator,' 1800, p. 48.

hall, for the same letter relates that one of the
Duchess's maids, travelling by the wagon, was
thrown out, run over, and died in consequence.[1]

At Bulstrode the new Duchess spent much of
her time; and here, as she says in one of her
letters, her amusements were 'all of the Rural
kind—Working, Spinning, Knotting, Drawing,
Reading, Writing, Walking, and picking Herbs
to put into an Herbal.'[2] These things, however,
by no means exhausted the list of her occupations. She was a clever turner both in wood and
ivory; she excelled in all kinds of fancy-work,
from 'sugar plum' chair-covers to embroidered
aprons; she was an expert in shell-flowers and
grotto-building; she delighted in feather-screens[3]
and cut-paper, in botany and natural history, in
curios and bric-à-brac of all sorts. Like a true
'Lady Bountiful,' she dabbled in the old-fashioned
remedies of the still-room[4]—decoctions of dande-
lion and penny-royal, infusions of poppy and

[1] Delany, 'Autobiography,' etc., 1861, ii, 23, 25.

[2] 'Elizabeth Montagu,' by Emily J. Climenson, 1906,
i, 27.

[3] Mrs. Montagu is usually associated with the famous
feather-hangings celebrated by Cowper ('Gentleman's
Magazine,' June 1788). But the idea originated with the
Duchess of Portland.

[4] These were the days when people took cowslip-wine

camomile. She talks of the tamarinds she has ordered for her ' apothecary's shop.' ' I am a *great doctor* [she says on another occasion] and have cured a poor boy of dropsy.' As a letter-writer, she was fluent and assiduous; but scarcely to be compared with some of the practised correspondents she had the good sense to attract and retain; and it is they who furnish us with the best idea of the life at Bulstrode. Foremost of these were the two Granvilles—Mary, then the widow of Mr. Pendarves and afterwards the better-known Mrs. Delany, and her sister, Anne, later Mrs.

for sleeplessness, added saffron to their tea against low spirits, and put goose-grass in their spring-porridge as ' good for the scurvy.' Conserve of marigold-flowers was reckoned a specific for trembling of the heart; while an approved recipe for toothache was trefoil, primrose leaves, and pounded yarrow. Viper broth was still used medicinally; and elixir of vitriol was recommended for asthma. Snails, also, were in favour, not as the table-delicacy referred to in Bramston's ' Man of Taste,' but to cure consumption. Some of the other remedies read oddly. Mrs. Delany speaks of a spider in a goose-quill, hung round a child's neck, as infallible in ague; and one of Mrs. Montagu's correspondents describes the lamentable case of an ancient Countess of Northampton who succumbed after a treatment of ' bouillon ' prepared from a cock which had been previously dosed for the purpose by Dr. Ward's celebrated pill.

D'Ewes; Mrs. (or rather Miss) Donnellan, a clever Irish friend of Swift and Richardson; Elizabeth Robinson, eventually the celebrated Mrs. Montagu, and Catherine, or Kitty Dashwood, the 'Delia-Neaera' of Hammond's lovesick 'Elegies.' Another was the daughter of John Law, the financier, a pretty, half-French Lady Wallingford. Like Johnson, the Duchess was fond of giving pet names to her favourites. Mrs. Pendarves was 'Pen' or 'Penny'; Miss Robinson, who was young and very volatile, 'Fidget'; Anne Granville, 'Pipkin'; Miss Dashwood, 'Dash.' Two of the group, 'Fidget' and 'Pen,' were accomplished chroniclers. Here is 'Fidget's' account of the Bulstrode 'carte du jour': 'We breakfast at 9, dine at 2, drink tea at 8, and sup at 10. In the morning we work or read. In the afternoon the same, walk from 6 till tea-time, and then write till supper. I think since we came down our despatches in numbers, tho' not in importance, have equalled those at the Secretary's Office. . . . The Duchess and I have been walking in the woods to-night, and feeding the pheasants in the menagerie. The late Duke had Macaws, Parrots, and all sorts of foreign birds flying in one of the woods; he built a house and kept people to wait upon them; there are now some birds in the house, and one Macaw, but most were destroyed in the Duke's minority.'[1]

This was in 1740. An earlier letter from the already indefatigable Mrs. Pendarves to her sister gives a variation of the picture. She is copying some drawings of Stonehenge lent her by Lord Oxford: 'They have employed me two mornings, and will two mornings more, so that my writing-hour is drove down to the evening. Well, I must drink coffee at five, and play with the little jewels—it is the ceremony of the house: then says the Duchess, "Don't go, Penny, till I have net one row in my cherry-net," which proves a hundred meshes, then comes some prater, asks her Grace a question; the arm suspended in the air forgets its occupation; she answers, and asks some other question in return—ten to one but a laugh is hatched, and once in a quarter of an hour the netting-work is remembered! With patience I await her solemn motions, and by half an hour after six we are in the dressing room [*i.e.* boudoir], armed with pen and ink, and the fair field prepared to receive the attack. Then comes Lady Elizabeth, Lady Harriet, and the noble Marquis [the three children]; after half an

[1] 'Elizabeth Montagu,' by Emily J. Climenson, 1906, i, 49-50.

hour's jumping, they are dismissed, and we soberly say " Now we will write our letters." In comes the Duke, " *the tea stays for the ladies* ": well, we must go, for there is no living at Bulstrode without four meals a day. . . ."[1]

The result is that it is eight before the correspondence is resumed, and ready for his Grace to frank. The children mentioned were Elizabeth, the eldest, afterwards first Marchioness of Bath; Henrietta, who became Countess of Stamford and Warrington; and William Henry (Lord Titchfield), eventually third Duke of Portland, at this date only a few months old. They were all engaging little people, and were presently to have an exemplary preceptress in the person of that accomplished Anglo-Saxon scholar, Miss (or Mrs.) Elizabeth Elstob, who, by the death of Caroline of Ansbach, had lost both her patron and her pension. It is strange that a lady who knew eight languages should not speak French—as Lord Oxford objected. But the Duchess sensibly decided that it would suffice if Miss Elstob contrived to teach her pupils English, cultivated their minds to the extent of their capacities, and instructed them 'in the principles of religion and virtue.'[2]

[1] Delany, ' Autobiography, etc.,' 1861, ii, 21-22.
[2] *Ibid.*, ii, 14.

She wished moreover to relieve them from the
frigid formalities and vexatious constraint under
which she herself had fretted as a child, and she
hoped that in this way they would grow up
affectionate and unaffected. Her plan must have
succeeded, since, some years later, Mrs. Pendarves
praises them for just these qualities. Miss Elstob
remained in the Portland family until her death
in 1756.

Apart from the periodical advent of visitors,
and the unwearied activities of the Duchess,
mingled with a good deal of miscellaneous reading
(in which the 'Decameron' alternated with
Clarke's Sermons, and Young's 'Night Thoughts'
corrected the levity of Cibber's 'Apology'), the
life at Bulstrode must have been, if not precisely
monotonous, at least exceedingly uniform. But
it was another-guess matter when the caravan,
with its four coaches-and-six, transported the
family to the Privy Garden, and the days were
filled with 'Operas, Park, Assemblies, Vaux Hall'
—when there were sittings at Hudson's or
Zincke's, and Handel oratorios and Caffarelli con-
certs—when Quin was acting Jaques superbly in
'As You Like It' and the French Dancers were
only rivalled in popularity by the new anon-
ymous novel of 'Pamela'—when there were

masquerades of Marylebone and balls at Leicester House. Perhaps the best illustration of what may be regarded as a decorous high-life 'frisk' of those days, is afforded by the record of an expedition to which the Duke and Duchess convened a select number of friends. The proceedings were reported independently by two of those present, whose accounts are here combined. The party consisted of the host and hostess; Mrs. Pendarves and Miss Donnellan; Lady Wallingford; Dr. Thomas Shaw, hereafter mentioned; Lord Dupplin, the Duchess's cousin, afterwards Earl of Kinnoul; and M. Achard, who had formerly been the Duke's tutor and was now his secretary and factotum. M. Achard, known familiarly in the family as 'Frère Bonaventure,' was of variable humour, a circumstance which led to his being nicknamed 'M. du *Poivre*,' or 'M. du *Miel*,' according to his dominant mood.[1] The intention was to visit all the shows between Whitehall and the Tower, and the sightseers accordingly set out at ten in two hackney coaches, ' stopping at everything that had a name.' The first halt was

[1] 'Elizabeth Montagu, by Emily J. Climenson, 1906, i, 62. But in a paper which, in September 1913, followed this in the 'National Review,' a much more favourable account is given of the Duke's quondam preceptor.

at the '*wild beasts*' in Covent Garden; but as
Mrs. Pendarves italicises the words, and Cun-
ningham makes no mention of any Covent Garden
menagerie, it is uncertain whether animals are
really to be understood. The next was at Saint
Bartholomew's Hospital, where, on the great
staircase, they inspect Mr. William Hogarth's
comparatively recent efforts in the Grand Style
of painting, the 'Good Samaritan' and the 'Pool
of Bethesda' (which Mrs. Pendarves misnames
the 'Impotent Man'). From 'Bart's' they pass
to the famous lapidary, Mr. Faulkner, where are
'abundance of fine things,' and they are instructed
in the cutting and polishing of pebbles. At
Surgeons' Hall, in Monkwell Street, they visit
the so-called picture by Holbein of Henry VIII
granting a Charter to the Barber Surgeons; after
which they proceed to the Tower and Mint to
recreate themselves with the assay of gold and
silver and the spectacle of lions and armour. Next
comes an excellent dinner at Pontack's in Ab-
church Lane, where you might have the best
Bordeaux wine procurable, and fare at five shil-
lings or a guinea a head, as it pleased your pocket.
After dining, they adjourned to the 'round
church in Stocks Market,'[1] that is, St. Stephen's,

[1] Delany, 'Autobiography, etc., 1861, ii, 82. In April

I

Walbrook, which, architectural experts notwithstanding, is assuredly one of Wren's most beautiful works. 'And so home to Whitehall'—as Pepys
would conclude, having passed—in Miss Donnellan's opinion—'a most agreeable day.' What
M. Achard thought on this occasion is not recorded. Let us trust he had not found the Pontack claret sophisticated ![1]

This 'notable expedition,' as Mrs. Pendarves
calls it, took place in April 1740, and must also
have been 'extraordinary' (in the eighteenth century sense), as there are no similar records. Nor
are they to be looked for, since the unchequered
life of the Duchess, like that of those fortunate
people who escape a history, presents, in the way
of definite chronicle, but few memorable mile-
stones. These may be at once enumerated. She
had, in due time, other children, besides those
mentioned already. In 1741 died Lord Harley,
who in 1724 had succeeded his father as second
Earl of Oxford. His death (Mrs. Pendarves does

1740, it may be added, the Stocks Market had been moved
to Farringdon Street, and the Mansion House was rising on
its site, which probably retained its old name for some time.

[1]   For sure those *Honest Fellows* have no knack
        Of putting off *stum'd Claret* for *Pontack*.

                    'The Hind and the Panther transvers'd,'
                            1687, p. 27.

not scruple to say it) was mainly due to intemperance, aggravated by the growing embarrassments which had obliged him, a year earlier, to part with Wimpole to Lord Hardwicke. His widow survived him until 1755, having sold the Harleian collection to the British Museum a short time before for £10,000. In 1762 the Duke of Portland died. There is not much about him in the correspondence of Mrs. Montagu or Mrs. Pendarves beyond the fact that he franked letters, and hunted three times a week in the season. But he had the care of a large estate, which must have kept him continually and usefully occupied. As for the Duchess—'les jours se suivent et se ressemblent.' Her mother's death added greatly to her possessions, not only in money but in pictures, miniatures, and all the heirlooms of the Nottinghamshire house, Welbeck Abbey. We hear of her continued occupations, her ruling passion for collecting, her improvements at Bulstrode, her bees, her tame hares and her pheasants, her botanical garden, and her intercourse with her friends. After Miss Robinson's marriage in 1742 to Mr. Montagu, the intimacy continued, and the husband and wife visited at Bulstrode. But in a few years, in consequence of some misunderstanding, it gradually fell off and was never renewed. On the other hand, the attachment to Mrs. Pendarves survived both that lady's second marriage to Dr. Delany and her second widowhood, the bond being only broken at last by the Duchess's death. It was at Bulstrode, when Mrs. Delany was more than seventy-three, that the idea first occurred to her of the famous paper flora which so delighted George III and Queen Charlotte, and which (by the bequest of Lady Llanover) still constitutes one of the glories of the Print Room at Bloomsbury. One day the old lady had casually cut out a scarlet geranium in paper of similar colour, with such verisimilitude that the Duchess mistook it for the real flower, and from that moment 'a new work was begun.' It was continued until 1782, and then only relinquished from fading eyesight.[1]

Hitherto we have said little of the men visitors to Bulstrode Park. One reason, and that almost suffices, is that there is not very much to say. The chosen associates of the Duchess were mostly of her own sex; or, if not, were particularly con-

[1] Delany, 'Autobiography, etc.,' 1862, v, 443; vi, 98. Cutting paper was a famous eighteenth-century ' accomplishment'; and Lady Andover is said to have excelled in minute figures and landscapes executed in this way. The art probably came over from Holland with William of Orange.

nected with her particular hobbies. Among these
latter came the botanist and conchologist, Dr.
Thomas Shaw, an explorer whose 'Travels in
Barbary and the Levant' obtained and deserved
the praise of Gibbon. The loud talk and hearty
laughter of this 'godfather of all Shell Fish' (as
Mrs. Montagu calls him) were often heard at
Bulstrode; and the Duchess is said to have given
him £600 to travel and collect shells for her, an
act in which she plainly showed herself Lord Harley's daughter. Others in this category were Mr.
(afterwards Sir) Joseph Banks and the Swede,
Solander, who, on their return from Cook's expedition of 1768-71, spent much of the summer
of 1772 at Bulstrode preparing an account of their
experiences. The 'simpling Macaroni,' as the
caricaturists called Solander, should have been at
his ease in the Duchess's herb-garden. Of purely
literary visitors the list is not large. One of the
earliest was doubtless Dr. Conyers Middleton,
whose 'Life of Cicero'—by no means an unimportant factor in the emancipation of biography
from the traditional models—was highly popular;
another, Lyttelton's friend, Gilbert West of
Wickham, who, besides his book on the Resurrec-
tion, had translated Pindar, and Lucian's 'Triumph of the Gout,' to which he was himself a

victim. West's taste for decoration cannot fail to have made him a 'persona grata' at Bulstrode. Dr. Zachary Grey, that laborious editor of 'Hudibras,' who, according to Fielding, quotes in his notes more than five hundred books *not* to be found in Mead's library, was also an occasional guest. But the most frequent and the most constant was Dr. Young, the author of the 'Night Thoughts'[1] and the 'Centaur not Fabulous,' whose conversational charm and gift of letter-writing are often extolled. Many of his epistles are printed or quoted from the originals at Longleat, in Mr. Henry C. Shelley's interesting 'Life and Letters of Edward Young' (Pitman, 1914). They are such as a Georgian ecclesiastic might be expected to address to a great lady who liked to be flattered discreetly; but although they are occasionally playful and ingenious, it can scarcely be claimed for them that they scintillate with the wit of the man who is supposed to have penned one of the neatest complimentary couplets in the language.[2] Of foreign 'littérateurs,' the most im-

[1] 'Night the Third. Narcissa'—was 'humbly Inscrib'd to her Gráce the Duchess of P——' in 1742

[2]   'Accept a miracle instead of wit:
    See two dull lines by STANHOPE's pencil writ.

Young's references to literature and his contemporaries

portant is that quaint (and diminutive) figure,
Father Pierre-François le Courayer, the Bene-
dictine translator of Sarpi's 'Council of Trent,'
who, after writing a book vindicating the Orders
of the English Church, had taken refuge in this
country in 1728. At Bulstrode, when he could
tear himself from Oxford, where Atterbury had
obtained for him a Doctor's degree, or from the
lodgings over Mrs. Chenevix's toy-shop at Charing
Cross, he was always welcome, as at many other
aristocratic houses which opened their doors to
him. Lastly, there must have been another comer,
Rousseau, of whose doings we should certainly
like to know more. He was in England in 1766-7
and spent much of his time at Wootton in Derby-
shire, near Calwich, where lived Mrs. Delany's
relative, Bernard Granville, to whom Jean Jacques
wrote several letters. Among these, Lady Llanover found one evidently intended for the Duchess,
as it refers to a title which—Rousseau says—she
had permitted him to assume, namely, that of

are of the scantest; but in one of these letters to the
Duchess he quotes (without owning them) his lines on
'Philander' from the second book of the 'Night Thoughts,
lines which have been suggested as prompting Goldsmith's
famous simile about the 'tall cliff' that 'midway leaves
the storm' in ll. 189-92 of the 'Deserted Village.'

'Herboriste de Madame la Duchesse de Portland.'
There was not much herbalizing possible in the
Privy-Garden at Whitehall; and it is only reasonable to conclude that the distinction must have
been conferred at Bulstrode.[1]

Concerning the Duchess's relations with some
of the other notabilities of her day, the record is
disappointingly barren. She knew, and had given
presents to, Horace Walpole; but beyond two
lines in a letter to George Montagu saying curtly
that she had dined at Strawberry Hill with Mrs.
Delany in June, 1770, there is no trace of intimacy. On the other hand, a few days later, Mrs.
Delany gives a fairly detailed account of an expedition she made to Hampton with her great
friend, and her great friend's daughter, Lady
Weymouth, in order to visit Garrick. That distinguished actor, though no doubt delighted, was
not dumbfounded. He did the honours of his
riverside villa[2] '*very respectfully*'; and Mrs.
Garrick—'*a wonderful creature*'—was propriety
itself, 'considering all circumstances relating to
her'—meaning, we suppose, that she had once
been an opera-dancer. The house, though 'sin-
gular,' had 'the look of belonging to *a genius*';

[1] Delany, 'Autobiography, etc.,' 1862, v, 98, 140.
[2] Recently sold, 'Times,' 21 April 1913.

the excellent dinner was 'nicely served'; and
the pretty garden sloping to the Thames 'very
well laid out, and planted for shade and shelter.'
They drank tea and coffee in Shakespeare's
Temple under Roubillac's statue (now in the
British Museum); and they duly admired the
famous Shakespeare chair.[1] Later on, Lady Weymouth's children walked into the garden, and
Garrick made himself as agreeable as he knew
how to do. The expedition must have been
wholly satisfactory; but Mrs. Delany's narrative
is marred by a patronizing note, hardly to be expected in Burke's typical fine lady. One would
like to hear Garrick's version of the proceedings;
or better, that of Mrs. Garrick—'considering all
circumstances relating to her.' Report says that
she was a person of marked social charm, and
devoted to her 'Davy.'[2]

But if Bulstrode patronized Hampton Villa,
Bulstrode in its turn was patronized by Gunnersbury House, for, two years later, Mrs. Delany

[1] Mrs. Delany calls this ' *Shakespeare's own chair* ';
but from her description it was obviously the mahogany
nondescript designed by Hogarth for Garrick, as president
of the Shakespeare Club. It afterwards belonged to the
late Baroness Burdett-Coutts. There is a sketch of it in
S. Ireland's 'Graphic Illustrations,' 1799, ii, 147.

[2] Delany, ' Autobiography, etc.,' 1862, v, 283-4.

gives an elaborate account of a 'gracious visit'
which, in the autumn of 1772 (the year of the
opening of the Pantheon), that indefatigable gad-
about, the Princess Amelia, paid the Duchess.
Here it is: 'All the comfortable sophas and
great chairs, all the piramids of books (adorning
almost every chair), all the tables and *even the
spinning-wheel* were banish'd for that day, and
the blew damask chairs set in prim form around
the room, only one arm'd chair placed in the
middle for her Royal Highness; she came in a
post coach and four, only attended by two footmen and a groom. . . . They were here by a qr
after one, conducted by the keeper, who met them
at the end of the common, and were brought
(not the common way), but thro' "*the bosom.*"
The D^{ss.} met her [the Princess] at the hall-door,
and I stood in the hall; when the Princess had
paid her complim^{ts} to her Grace, she came up
directly to me and said many civil things wch
I hope I answer'd properly. She was so easy,
good-humoured, and entertaining that I was glad
I had not absented myself. She was delighted
with the place and her entertainment, which was
magnificent and pollish'd to the last degree, yet
everything conducted with the utmost ease. The
Princess went all over the house and garden, but

insisted upon the Dss. of P. and my not attending her there, only her ladies. We dined at three, and she had a polite attention to every ingenious ornament on the table and you may be sure Mr. Leiver's [the chef's?] ingenuity, &c., was *not idle* on this occasion. After dinner she would see my own apartments, and made me display all my frippery works, all which she graciously commended; we then adjourned into the library, and at seven the Princess return'd to Gunnersbury by moonlight.' [1]

The graciousness of Gunnersbury House was, however, nothing compared with the amenity of Windsor Castle, when, on a memorable day in August 1776, 'Great George our King' and Queen Charlotte drank tea at Bulstrode, and Mrs. Delany (in her own words) was 'produced among the antiquities.' Between six and seven their serene Majesties arrived in a chaise and pair, bringing with them Lady Weymouth. The house, as before, had been turned upside down to receive them, and 'the drawing room divested of every comfortable circumstance.' The royal visitors 'took notice, and admired everything'— especially the Duchess and the 'hortus siccus.' The intercourse thus opened was afterwards often

---

[1] Delany, 'Autobiography, etc.,' 1862, iv, 455-6.

renewed. In August 1778, on the Prince of Wales's birthday, the King and Queen, with eight children and attendants, fifty in all, breakfasted at Bulstrode. Mrs. Delany was again 'commandeered,' her paper flowers were inspected by a larger party than before, and the good-humoured royalties perambulated the entire house, admiring the pictures, the china closet and the numberless curiosities. They then had chocolate in the gallery, and the King carried his affability to the extent of handing Mrs. Delany a chair. This invasion of Bulstrode was followed by a return visit to Windsor, as Mrs. Delany had expressed a desire to see the entire royal family. It came off the next day, when the Duchess and her interesting friend went to the Castle, and were received with much simple cordiality, including the privilege of seeing the Prince of Wales and the Bishop of Osnaburg (Prince Frederick) dance a minuet in the music-room at the Queen's house. Mrs. Delany's account of these proceedings (she was now nearing eighty) is something too much in the worm-and-star style, though the narrative gives a pleasant impression of the genuine courtesy and unconventional kindness of 'Farmer George' and his wife. In a later letter there is a pretty picture of the King,

carrying about in his arms his youngest-born, the
short-lived Prince Octavius; and in another, later
still, although, as a preliminary, the illustrious
guests were escorted through Bulstrode Park with
blazing flambeaux, and the Duchess lighted in
their honour the great chandelier which had not
been lit for twenty years, the Queen chatted with
her hostess on a sofa, the Princess Royal played
the harpsichord while the Prince of Wales sang;
and the company consumed the refreshments as
naturally as if they had been hungry citizens in a
supper-box at Vauxhall.

So much for royalty. It would be interesting
to connect the Duchess with her illustrious contemporary, the 'great Cham of Literature.' But
beyond the fact that, in the year of the Gordon
Riots, Dr. Johnson met her Grace at one of Mrs.
Vesey's 'Babels,' Boswell makes no reference to
that 'fair conjunction.' On the other hand, the
'Diary' of Miss Burney for January 1783 contains
a vivacious sketch of an interview which, greatly
to her satisfaction, the much-flattered author of
the then recently published 'Cecilia' had with
the Duchess at Mrs. Delany's house in St. James's
Place. Miss Burney discovered much 'sweetness
and dignity and intelligence' in her new friend.
The Duchess was wonderfully condescending, at

once accepting Fanny's opinion of Mrs. Siddons as final. She further delighted her hearer by announcing that, despite an antipathy to five volumes, she had read ' Cecilia ' three times—a commendation enhanced by the supplementary declaration that she had never been able to get through more than a few letters of ' Clarissa ' or ' Sir Charles Grandison.' But over ' Cecilia ' both she and Mrs. Delany had cried—oh! how they had cried! Then followed discussion of the ' dramatis personæ,' to which Mrs. Chapone (who had accompanied Miss Burney) contributed the familiar vindication of the eccentric Briggs. It had been asserted, in a mixed company, that there could be no such character. Whereupon ' a poor little mean city man who was there, started up and said, " But there is though, for I'se one myself." ' After this, and some further laudation, Miss Burney's sensitive modesty could ' hear no more.' Indeed, she has been obliquely accused (by the ever-suspicious Croker, who distrusted reported dialogues) of hearing more than was actually uttered. But she could scarcely have invented this particular episode.[1]

The Duchess Dowager of Portland, as she had become since the marriage of the third Duke in

[1] ' Burney Diary,' 1904, ii, 197-202.

1766, died at Bulstrode on the 17th of July 1785, in her seventy-second year. Her life, it may be gathered, was not fruitful of incident, and therefore lends itself but little to chronological treatment. From the dispersed sources consulted for this paper, she emerges indistinctly as a shadowy but beneficent presence,[1] with a genius for friendship and a taste for collecting—a taste which, in her later years, does not seem to have entirely commended itself to her expectant and embarrassed heirs. In April 1786, the ' Portland Museum,' announced in auctioneer phraseology as 'known throughout Europe,' and consisting of 'shells, corals, minerals, insects, birds' eggs, agates, crystals, china, snuff-boxes, coins, medals, seals, prints, drawings, jewels, and precious stones,' was sold by Skinner and Co. at her Grace's 'late dwelling house in Privy-Garden.' The sale occupied about thirty days, and included 4,156 lots. One of the buyers was Horace Walpole, who secured a head in basalt of Jupiter Serapis, and an

[1] Writing in August 1742, Lady Mary Wortley Montagu says of her daughter, Lady Bute: ' I am very glad she continues her intimacy with the Duchess of Portland, whose company will never injure her either by advice or example ' (Paston's ' Lady Mary Wortley Montagu,' 1907, 406).

illuminated Book of Psalms, both of which he forthwith installed in the Beauclerk closet at Strawberry. Another item was a unique set of Hollar's engravings, in thirteen folio volumes. This fetched £385, but the prices generally were far below what they would have been in our time. Rembrandt etchings, for example, went for 28*s.*; Chelsea China (28 pieces) for 30*s.* The gem of the sale was the blue and white glass Vase, or Sepulchral Urn, thought to have once held the ashes of Alexander Severus, which had been discovered near Rome in a sarcophagus under the Monte del Grano. Until 1770 this marvel of the ceramic art had remained in the possession of the Barberini family, being subsequently acquired by Sir William Hamilton, British Plenipotentiary at Naples, from whom, through his niece, Miss Hamilton, one of Queen Charlotte's ladies-in-waiting, the Duchess purchased it for £1,800. Henceforth it became known as the Hamilton or Portland Vase. At the sale it was bought in by the third Duke for £1,029, and deposited by his son in the British Museum. Here it was smashed to pieces in February 1845 by a drunken workman; and was afterwards most ingeniously and successfully pieced together by Mr. Thomas Doubleday.

THE GORDON RIOTS

When the rude rabble's watch-word was—destroy,
And blazing London seem'd a second Troy.

COWPER's 'Table Talk,' 1781.

LORD GEORGE GORDON is one of
those ambiguous historical personages who,
for a brief period, flash into sudden significance,
and then, having contrived to do incalculable
harm, fade away again as suddenly. Their intentions may have been good, though their methods were mistaken; but as individuals they lie
so much on the border line that it is difficult to
determine whether they are more sane than mad
—more fanatic than lunatic. The difficulty of
discriminating is not diminished by the absence
of biographical data; and as regards Lord George's
early life, the recorded facts are only moderately
enlightening. He was the third son of the third
Duke of Gordon, and was born in London in
December 1751. Like Pope's Molly Lepel, he
received a military commission when scarcely out
of his cradle; but he ultimately entered the Navy
from Eton as a midshipman. He served on the

K

American station, rising to be a lieutenant in
March 1772. Then, being disappointed of a ship
by the First Lord of the Admiralty, Lord Sandwich, he quitted the Service. Having thus declined to become a Howe or a Hawke, he is
next heard of as a candidate for Inverness-shire.
This he contested with General Fraser (eldest
son of Hogarth's Lord Lovat), who, finding his
rival's faculty for speaking Gaelic and giving
balls with attractive Highland partners made him
a too formidable antagonist, judged it prudent to
purchase for him, from Lord Melbourne, the seat
of Ludgershall in Wiltshire, for which he was returned in 1774. Concerning his senatorial career,
little is related except that he made himself con-
spicuous, if not notorious, for his impartiality in
attacking both the Ins and the Outs, and for his
denunciations of the Roman Catholics. Finally,
in June 1780 his name is inseparably connected
with the 'No Popery' Riots.

The story of the five days' disturbances, which
practically paralysed London and almost amounted
to a temporary Reign of Terror, requires no long
introduction. In 1778, when the toleration
which the different Governments of Europe
were extending to their peaceable Roman Catholic
subjects was gradually beginning to obtain in

England, Sir George Savile, one of the most open-minded and upright of philanthropists—in whom some critics have recognized the lineaments of Goldsmith's 'Mr. Burchell'—introduced a Bill to relieve Roman Catholics in this country from certain civil disabilities and penalties to which they were liable under an Act of William of Orange. That monarch, it was said, had never really approved it; and from lapse of time and altered conditions it had become not only unnecessary but unjust. Those whom Savile's measure immediately concerned, welcomed it warmly; and the Bill was carried in both Houses without a division. Then came the question of extending its provisions to Scotland. But here, at once, difficulties arose with the Presbyterians. The provincial synods hastened to form adverse Protestant associations; and the agitation thus created was assiduously fanned by sermons, pamphlets, and newspaper paragraphs. As a result, at Edinburgh and Glasgow serious riots took place, in which Mass-houses were burned, and much Roman Catholic property was destroyed. So sinister and determined was the opposition, that the authorities decided to hold their hands; and as far as Scotland was concerned, legislation was abandoned.

In England, however, where, for some time, a
'No Popery' movement had been simmering in
the public Press, these proceedings in Scotland
naturally produced a reaction. A London 'Protestant Association' was at once set on foot, and
Lord George Gordon, who had been at the head
of a similar body in North Britain, was elected
president. He attended the initial deliberations
regularly; and on Monday, 29 May, assembled by
advertisement an extraordinary meeting in Coachmakers' Hall, Foster Lane, Cheapside, to con-
sider the best method of presenting a petition to
Parliament for the repeal of Savile's Act. Taking
for his pretext the success of resistance in North
Britain, he delivered a 'long inflammatory har-
angue.' In consequence, a unanimous resolution
was passed, that, on the following Friday, the
entire Protestant Association, distinguished by
blue knots or ribbons, should meet in St. George's-
Fields (a waste space on the Surrey side of the
Thames, where the whirligig of Time has now
erected a Roman Catholic Cathedral) and accom-
pany its president to the House of Commons.
Upon this, Lord George announced that if less
than twenty thousand of his fellow citizens attended, he would not present the petition; and he
further suggested that, for the better preservation

of order, they should group themselves in different divisions.

On 2 June, the day fixed, these arrangements were carried out, with an exactitude which reflects considerable credit on the executive of the Protestant Association. Starting from St. George's-Fields at noon, one party, led by Gordon himself, and preceded by the petition—a huge roll of parchment said to contain a hundred and twenty thousand signatures—crossed the river at Westminster. Another section made its way by Blackfriars; a third by London Bridge. About half-past two, the whole body had simultaneously reached Palace Yard, an event which they signalized by a 'general shout.' Up to this time their progress had been quiet and decorous; but it soon became evident that their ranks had been largely recruited on the road by many undesirable sympathizers of the lowest class, and that the motley cohort which accompanied Gordon to the very entrance of the Commons, and surged after him into the Lobby, must have included not a few spurious 'blue cockades,' whose proclivities were plainly rather to lawless action than passive protest. These last speedily began to hustle and maltreat the Members as they arrived, particularly if they happened to be Peers, constraining them to cry

'No Popery'—to assume the Protestant badge
—to promise to support the repeal of the Act.
They even attempted to force the doors of the
House, all the approaches to which they effectually blockaded. In Parliament Street, the Archbishop of York was hissed and hooted. The
Lord President of the Council, old Lord Bathurst,
was violently assaulted and kicked; Lord Mansfield ('clarum et venerabile nomen!'), who had
been instrumental in acquitting a Popish priest,
not only had the glasses and panels of his coach
beaten in, but narrowly escaped with his life.
The hat of Lord North, the Premier, was seized,
cut to pieces and the fragments sold to the spec-
tators; [1] the Duke of Northumberland was robbed
of his watch; the Bishop of Lichfield's gown was
torn to tatters; and the Bishop of Lincoln, a
brother of the unpopular Lord Chancellor Thur-
low—his carriage-wheels having been wrenched
off—was only saved in a half-fainting condition
by seeking shelter in a neighbouring house,
whence he departed in disguise over the adjoining roofs. Other high dignitaries and politicians
fared no better. Lord Townshend, then Master-
General of the Ordnance, and Lord Hillsborough,
a Secretary of State, having been grossly insulted,

[1] Angelo's 'Reminiscences,' 1830, ii, 146.

lost those ' honours of their heads,' their silk bags, and entered the House with their hair hanging loose; while Lord Stormont, another Secretary of State, whose equipage was literally battered to pieces, after remaining helpless for nearly half an hour in the hands of the rabble, was at last extricated by the courageous intervention of a friendly bystander. Lord Boston was so long detained by his assailants that, at one time, it was proposed by his brother Peers to sally out in a body to his assistance. Similar outrages were suffered by Lord Willoughby de Broke, Lord St. John, and Lord Dudley, while Welbore Ellis, the Treasurer of the Navy, got free with the utmost hazard by taking sanctuary at the Westminster Guildhall, the windows of which were forthwith smashed, the doors demolished, and the Justice and constables ejected.

Inside the House—as soon as opportunity offered, for the state of things outside naturally engrossed considerable attention—Lord George, in due form, presented his petition, demanding its immediate consideration. During the heated debate that took place he repeatedly came to the top of the gallery-stairs to acquaint his supporters in the Lobby with the course taken by the discussion, and to denounce to them those—North

and Burke among others—who opposed his motion. By several of the members these ill-advised
utterances were warmly resented. Walpole's
friend, General Conway, publicly rebuked the
reckless orator, whom others threatened with
personal violence; and Colonel Murray,[1] his relative, appearing suddenly at his side, declared,
in a voice audible to those below, that he would
run his sword into Lord George's body the instant
any of his Lordship's 'rascally adherents' pre-
sumed to enter the House. Eventually the Commons, courageously declining to be overawed by
numbers—and the postulated twenty had now
grown to about sixty thousand—adjourned consideration of the petition to Tuesday, 6 June.
The dissatisfied concourse were therefore left to
console themselves with their leader's optimistic
assurance that he had no doubt King George the
Third, being a gracious monarch, 'would send to
his Ministers to repeal the Act when he saw the
confusion it created.'[2]   In the meantime Lord

[1] In the 'Annual Register' and 'Barnaby Rudge'
this name is given as Gordon. But in Walpole's 'Letters,'
the 'Gentleman's Magazine,' and 'Notes and Queries' it
is Murray—*i.e.* Colonel James Murray of Strowan, Member
for Perthshire, and uncle to the Duke of Athol.

[2] Erskine's 'Speeches,' 1810, i, 63.

North had contrived to summon the Guards. But it was nearly nine before they made their appearance, and the vast assembly which had kept the two Houses besieged for many hours of a stifling June day, gradually dispersed. Yet, though the majority broke up in Westminster, there were many of them still deliberately bent on mischief; and these—following the Scottish precedent— forthwith repaired to the Romish chapels of the Bavarian and Sardinian Ministers in Golden Square and Lincoln's Inn Fields, which—to use their own word — they 'gutted,' and burned, carrying away silver lamps, vestments, and appointments. Tardily, as before, the troops arrived, and some thirteen of the rioters were lodged in the Savoy.

With the scenes that ensued, it will be best to deal in the time-table fashion adopted by Dr. Johnson to Mrs. Thrale. On Saturday, the 3rd, the rioters remained quiet; but on the afternoon of Sunday, the 4th, they assembled in force to attack the chapels and dwellings of the Roman Catholics in and about Moorfields. Altars, pulpits, pews, and furniture were ruthlessly broken up, nothing being left but bare walls. On Monday, the 5th, kept as the King's birthday, the mob paraded as far as Lord George's house in Welbeck

Street, taking with them their spoils and trophies, which they burned in the then-adjacent fields. They afterwards made their way to Wapping and Smithfield, intent on similar depredations; but directing their efforts more especially against those who had given evidence with respect to the prisoners taken on the previous Friday. Sir George Savile, the introducer of the Act of 1778, was also singled out for retribution. He had been wary enough to remove his plate; but his historic house on the north side of Leicester Square was completely stripped, its contents set fire to in the inclosure, and its iron railings converted into weapons of offence.

On the same day, in spite of the fact that the now contrite Protestant Association issued a handbill, signed by its President, deprecating 'all unconstitutional Proceedings,' the Guards, who took three of the aforementioned prisoners from Bow Street to Newgate, were on their return pelted by the populace. On Tuesday, the 6th, the two Houses, the Tower, and St. James's Palace were all in charge of the troops; but Lord Sandwich, driving to Westminster, was nevertheless assaulted. His coach was wrecked, he himself was cut about the face, and the Light Horse had the greatest difficulty in protecting

him from further ill-usage. In the evening a
punitive party of the rioters demolished the house
in St. Martin's Street of Justice Hyde, who had
led the soldiers to Palace Yard. Between six and
seven another party set out, by way of Long
Acre and Holborn, for Newgate, bent on releasing
their captured comrades. On the refusal of
Boswell's friend, Mr. Akerman, the head keeper,
to deliver them up without authority, they at
once attacked and burned his house, subsequently
piling his blazing furniture against the door of
the prison, which, like the house, was speedily
in flames, and the prisoners, some three hundred
in number, including four under immediate sentence of death, were set at liberty, of course
swelling the ranks of the malcontents. Other
outrages followed these. Justice Cox's house in
Great Queen Street was burned; as also that in
Bow Street of Sir John Fielding. At Clerkenwell
Green the so-called New Prison was broken
open, and the prisoners turned out; after which
a more desperate gang attacked Lord Mansfield's
famous mansion in the corner of Bloomsbury
Square. Beginning by breaking the doors and
windows, they went on to fling the contents of
the rooms into the street, where large fires were
ready lighted to receive them. They then burned

the valuable library, some thousand volumes, including 'many capital manuscripts, mortgages, papers, and other deeds.' Priceless pictures [1] and sumptuous wearing apparel were also consigned to the flames, and the choice vintages of the cellars 'plentifully bestowed' on the populace. The Guards arriving, the Riot Act was read; and there was some half-hearted firing on the part of the soldiers. Nothing, however, could check the fury of the rabble, who literally pulled the building down, burning even the out-houses and stables, so that, in a short time, the whole was entirely consumed. Lord and Lady Mansfield had fortunately made their exit by a back door before the rioters got in. Not satisfied with what they had done, however, a party of miscreants set out to destroy his Lordship's country seat at Caen Wood, Hampstead. But here, happily, they were forestalled, the house being protected by the Militia.

Lord Mansfield's household goods were still blazing fiercely at one o'clock on the morning of

[1] Malone thought these included Pope's solitary effort at portraiture in oil. But this must have been safe at Caen Wood; for Pope's copy of Kneller's Betterton was exhibited at the National Portrait Exhibition in 1867 by the Earl of Mansfield (No. 61).

Wednesday 7 June—the blackest day in the record. In the forenoon the mob had the 'infernal
humanity' to give notice that they intended to
burn the Fleet, the King's Bench, and other
buildings, specifying in particular the premises of
Mr. Thomas Langdale, a well-known Roman
Catholic distiller in Holborn, next to Barnard's
Inn. This plan of campaign was carried out so
punctually that at nightfall some six-and-thirty
fires are said to have been visible from London
Bridge, burning simultaneously in different
quarters of the city. At Mr. Langdale's the
scene was 'horrible beyond description.' His
vaults were stored with vast quantities of un-
rectified spirit which ran from the started casks
in torrents down the street; and, when ignited,
added to the fury of the flames. Numbers of
rioters and onlookers drank greedily of the liquor;
and were either suffocated at once or burned to
death in a state of stupor. Others were buried in
the ruins of the falling houses. But by this time
the palsied authorities, galvanized into decision
by the timely firmness of George the Third, had
recovered from their deplorable lethargy. Detach-
ments of Regulars and Militia came pouring into
the Metropolis at many points. Gradually the
field of action was contracted; and the insurgents

were effectually checked. Attempts on the Pay
Office at Whitehall, and the Bank of England [1]
(where Alderman Wilkes and Gibbon's friend,
Col. Holroyd, afterwards Lord Sheffield, led the
defending forces) were successfully repulsed; and
by Thursday, the 8th, though the shops continued
shut, and business remained at a standstill, it was
plain that the protracted misrule had reached its
close, and there was no longer anything to fear.
Seventy-two private houses and four public jails
had been destroyed.[2] Two hundred and eighty-
five of the rioters are said to have been killed
outright by the military; one hundred and seventy-
three were wounded; fifty-nine were capitally
convicted, and twenty-one of these were afterwards
executed. But of those who died from intoxica-

---

[1] In attacking the Bank of England the rioters were
led by a brewer's boy on a powerful dray-horse, which was
caparisoned with fetters taken from Newgate. Dickens has
remembered this in Chap. 67 of 'Barnaby Rudge,' where
such a charger is ridden by Hugh of the Maypole. Another
instance of his minute study of his material is to be found
in the death of the blind man, Stagg, in Chap. 69, who is
killed by the soldiers, and runs full forty yards after he is
hit. This is plainly suggested by a passage in the ' Annual
Register,' 1780, p. 261, describing the destruction of the
toll-gates at Blackfriars. 'One man, who was shot, ran
thirty or forty yards before he dropped.'

[2] 'Annual Register,' 1780, p. 281.

tion or other causes, the number was never accurately ascertained. A large number of the escaped
prisoners—it should be added—were speedily re-
taken, and placed once more in confinement.

In the first half of the last century there must
have been not a few who, as children, remembered, with Raimbach the engraver, the roar of
the rioters rushing through the streets and calling
to all good citizens to illuminate—nay, there
must have been those living who, like Walpole's
printer Kirgate, had actually seen dead bodies
lying by empty casks in Holborn. Many trustworthy eye-witnesses have left their impressions
of this terrible time; and most of the contemporary memoir writers refer to one or other of the
incidents which came under their especial notice.
Walpole, Gibbon, Burke, Johnson, Susan Burney,
Crabbe, Wraxall, Angelo—all contribute their
quota, confirmatory or otherwise, to the body of
evidence. To Walpole, the arch-priest of the
'nouvelles à la main,' who scribbles off daily
letters to Mann and Mason and Lady Ossory on
the reigning theme, one naturally turns first,
though much of what he has to say is the merest
hand-to-mouth gossip (including, of course, Selwyn's latest 'mot' thereon) which to-morrow will
contradict, and it is safer to trust to what he has

actually seen than to those 'first reports' he has
heard. Personally he had 'disliked and condemned
the repeal of the Popish statutes,' but he was
equally averse from reformation by massacre;
and for him Lord George is a 'lunatic,' an 'arch-
incendiary,' the 'ruffian apostle that preached up
the storm,' etc. He confirms generally the occurrences in Palace Yard, decorating them, of
course, in his own inimitable way; and he also
makes mention more than once of the intervention of Colonel Murray. Lord Mansfield (whom
he disapproved) he describes as 'quivering on the
woolsack like an aspen,' which, seeing that he was
a septuagenarian who had been in imminent
danger, was not unnatural. Of the burning of
the Chapels on the same day, Walpole writes to
Lady Ossory on 3 June: 'The mob forced the
Sardinian Minister's chapel in Lincoln's Inn
Fields, and gutted it. He saved nothing but two
chalices; lost the silver lamps, &c., and the
benches being tossed into the street, were food
for a bonfire, with the blazing brands of which
they set fire to the inside of the chapel, nor, till
the Guards arrived, would suffer the engines to
play. My cousin, T[homas] Walpole, fetched
poor Madam Cordon,[1] who was ill, and guarded

---

[1] The Sardinian Minister was the Marquis de Cordon.

her in his house till three in the morning, when all was quiet.'

The Chapel of St. Anselm and St. Cecilia was the oldest Roman Catholic place of worship in London, which was probably why it was selected for destruction by the wirepullers of the mob. As a connoisseur, Walpole should have regretted the loss of its beautiful altar-piece by the Chevalier Casali, alleged to have cost £2,500. To Count Haslang, the Bavarian envoy, he is unsympathetic: 'Old Haslang's Chapel was broken open and plundered; and, as he is a prince of smugglers as well as Bavarian Minister, great quantities of run tea and contraband goods were found in his house. This one cannot lament; and still less, as the old wretch has for these forty years usurped a hired house, and, though the proprietor for many years has offered to remit his arrears of rent, he will neither quit the house nor pay for it.'[1]

Of the depredations of Sunday, Walpole says little, as he had returned to Strawberry to avoid the official Birthday (Monday the 5th), and for the next occurrences we must go to a fresh witness, Fanny Burney's lively sister, Susan, then resident with her family in Sir Isaac Newton's old house, No. 1, St. Martin's Street, Leicester

[1] Walpole to Sir Horace Mann, 5 June 1780.

L

Square, the Observatory of which afforded exceptional opportunities for surveying the scenes in their immediate neighbourhood.[1] From this coign of vantage they saw the whole of Leicester Square lighted up by Sir George Savile's burning property. 'They [the mob] had piled up the furniture in the midst of the Square, and had

---

[1] 'Newton House,' once No. 1, and latterly No. 35, St. Martin's Street, the residence from 1710 to 1725 of Sir Isaac Newton; and from 1774, and many years subsequently, of Dr. Charles Burney, the musician, is now pulled down. The 'Observatory,' to which Susan Burney refers, existed in 1778, since Fanny Burney tells us expressly that her father went to the expense of practically reconstructing it after the hurricane of that year. Parts of her first novel, 'Evelina,' were written in this 'square turret.' It is consolatory to learn from a letter of Mr. Hugh Phillips to the 'Times' of 4 December 1913, that this historic dwelling has not fallen a prey to the housewrecker; and that it has been removed 'in sections carefully packed and numbered,' to Hitchin, where its re-erection is contemplated. That this may come to pass is devoutly to be wished, if only to justify Lord Macaulay's too-sanguine prediction in the 'Edinburgh Review' for January 1843, that the building would 'continue to be well known as long as our island retains any trace of civilisation.' Meanwhile a useful memorial of it exists in Miss Constance Hill's pleasant volume entitled 'The House in St. Martin's Street,' 1907, to which we are indebted for our extracts from Susan Burney's unpublished Diary.

NO. I ST. MARTIN'S STREET

(FROM A PHOTOGRAPH)

forced Sir George's servant to bring them a
candle to set fire to it. They would doubtless
have set the house itself on fire [also] had not the
Horse and Foot Guards prevented [their doing
so].' This was early on Monday, the 5th. Next
day came the retributory burning of Justice
Hyde's, which was in St. Martin's Street itself.[1]
'From our windows we saw them throw chairs,
tables, cloathes, in short everything the house
contained, into the street, and as there was too
much furniture for *one* fire, they made several. I
counted six of these fires, which reached from
the bottom of the street up to the crossing which
separates Orange and Blue Cross Streets. Such a
scene I never before beheld! As it grew dusk,
the wretches who were involved in smoak and
covered with dust, with the flames glaring upon
them, . . . seemed like so many infernals. . . .

[1] The 'Gentleman's Magazine' says Hyde's house was
in Lisle Street. But Lisle Street lies north of Leicester
Square; and Susan Burney places the house towards the
bottom of 'our street,' *i.e.* St. Martin's Street on the
southern side. Lisle Street has, however, its memories of
these troublous days, since Francis Wheatley's great picture of the Riots, being too large to be removed, was destroyed here at a fire in the house of James Heath, who
engraved it for Boydell (Edwards's 'Anecdotes of Painters,'
1808, p. 269).

'One thing was remarkable and convinced me that the mob was secretly directed by somebody above themselves:—they brought an engine with them, and while they pulled Hyde's house to pieces and threw everything they found into the flames, they ordered the engine to play on the neighbouring houses to prevent their catching fire.' [1]

Early that morning Mrs. Burney, Susan's stepmother, had seen Burke pass through St. Martin's Street, beset by a crowd who wished to extort from him a promise that he would vote for the repeal of the Act. 'My mother . . . heard him say: "I beseech you, gentlemen; gentlemen, I beg——".' Finally he was obliged to draw his sword in order to free himself from their importunities. He was lucky to escape. He had been denounced with North by Lord George at Westminster, as opposing the repeal; and if his house in Charles Street, St. James's Square, had not been stoutly garrisoned by sixteen soldiers, it would probably have shared the fate of that of Sir George Savile.

One of the diarist's entries illustrates the difficulties of the military. An Ensign and thirty Foot Guards marched into the street, and after a

[1] 'The House in St. Martin's Street,' 1907, 257.

few words to the rioters from the officer, marched out again, 'the mob shouting and clapping the soldiers on their backs as they passed.' The soldiers were as unwilling to use force as the magistrates were to send for the soldiers; and Walpole mentions a brother-in-law of Lord George, who had 'to conceal himself' because he had given orders to fire at Bloomsbury Square. Such a state of things Johnson had foreseen four years before when he said: 'The characteristick of our own government at present is imbecility. The magistrate dare not call the guards for fear of being hanged. The guards will not come, for fear of being given up to the blind rage of popular juries.'[1]

At night-time the watchers from the St. Martin's Street Observatory saw the flames ascending from Sir John Fielding's house and office in Bow Street; from Newgate; and from Lord Mansfield's. Concerning this last, there is not much to add, save that Parson Warner, Selwyn's chaplain and Thackeray's Sampson, found, or professed to have found, a page of Virgil from the famous library—the 'letter'd store' of which Cowper wrote—fluttering in the enclosure. 'Sunt lacrimae rerum'—was the

[1] Hill's 'Boswell's Johnson,' 1887, iii, 46.

legend on this fugitive fragment. Many similar relics, charred and stained, were for a long time preserved in Caen Wood; but 'silver-tongued Murray' is said to have regretted most of all the loss of his manuscript of a speech on the privilege of Parliament which he considered contained all the law and all the eloquence he possessed. To this, possibly, Cowper intended to refer in the neat copy of verses he sent to William Unwin:

> And MURRAY sighs o'er Pope and Swift,
>   And many a treasure more,
> The well-judg'd purchase and the gift
>   That grac'd his letter'd store.
>
> *Their* pages mangled, burnt, and torn,
>   The loss was *his alone*;
> But ages yet to come shall mourn
>   The burning of *his own*.

Sir John Fielding had also to lament the destruction of his furniture, effects, and 'writings'—a lament with which posterity may fairly sympathize, as they probably included some of the rare letters and MSS. of the great novelist who was his half-brother and predecessor. But if details are scanty as to Bow Street and Bloomsbury Square, they are abundant concerning the burning of Newgate. George Crabbe, the poet,

who, with three pounds in his pocket, had come
to London in the previous April to seek his
fortune, was still seeking it when, wandering
aimlessly homeward to his lodging near the
Royal Exchange, he turned out of Ludgate Hill
at about half-past seven on Tuesday evening (the
6th) to discover the mob already occupied in
firing Mr. Akerman's house: 'As I was standing
near the spot [he writes in his journal to Miss
Elmy, the Mira of his affections], there approached
another body of men, I suppose 500, and Lord
George Gordon in a coach, drawn by the mob
towards Alderman Bull's [the seconder of his
motion in the House of Commons], bowing as
he passed along. He is a lively looking young
man in appearance, and nothing more, though
just now the reigning hero.[1] By eight o'clock,
Akerman's house was in flames. I went close to
it, and never saw anything so dreadful. The
prison was, as I said, a remarkably strong building; but, determined to force it, they broke the
gates with crows and other instruments, and
climbed up the outside of the cell part, which
joins the two great wings of the building, where
the felons were confined; and I stood where I

[1] This was on the 6th when he left the House of
Commons. See *post*, p. 156.

plainly saw their operations. They broke the roof, tore away the rafters, and having got ladders they descended. . . . Flames all around them, and a body of soldiers expected, they defied and laughed at all opposition. The prisoners escaped. I stood and saw about twelve women and eight men ascend from their confinement to the open air, and they were conducted through the streets in their chains. . . . You have no conception of the frenzy of the multitude. This being done, and Akerman's house now a mere shell of brickwork, they kept a store of flame there for other purposes. It became red hot, and the doors and windows appeared like the entrances to so many volcanoes. With some difficulty they then fired the debtor's prison—broke the doors—and they, too, all made their escape. Tired of the scene, I went home. . . .'[1]

At eleven o'clock he returned to find Newgate 'open to all,' for the incendiaries had transferred their operations to Bloomsbury Square. Another spectator of the attack upon Newgate was Henry Angelo, the fencing-master, who, hiring for sixpence a garret-window opposite, had a full view of the whole—the first onslaught with pick-axes and sledge hammers, the breaking open of the

[1] Crabbe's 'Works,' 1834, i, 83.

debtor's-door, the subsequent rising of smoke from different points, and 'a new species of jail delivery.' 'The captives marched out with all the honours of war, accompanied by a musical band of rattling fetters,' which Angelo presently heard being knocked off in the neighbouring houses.[1] Next day (the 7th) Dr. Johnson who, at Bolt Court, was not far off, visited the ruins: 'On Wednesday [he writes to Mrs. Thrale] I walked with Dr. Scot [afterwards Lord Stowell] to look at Newgate, and found it in ruins, with the fire yet glowing. As I went by, the Protestants were plundering the Sessions-house at the Old Bailey. There were not, I believe, a hundred; but they did their work at leisure, in full security without sentinels, without trepidation, as men lawfully employed, in full day. Such is the cowardice of a commercial place.'[2]

And then he goes on to enumerate the incidents of 'black Wednesday,' when one might watch, as Walpole watched from the roof of Gloucester House in Upper Grosvenor Street, 'the glare of conflagration fill the sky;' and listen hourly to fresh tidings of new enormities at Blackfriars and Holborn.

[1] Angelo's ' Reminiscences, 1830, ii, 147-8.
[2] Hill's ' Johnson's Letters,' 1892, ii, 169.

With the 7th came the King's Proclamation, and the belated issue of General Orders authorizing the military to 'use force for dispersing the illegal and tumultuous assemblies of the people.' Wraxall, who, though he mixes up his dates, seems to have witnessed the burning of Lord Mansfield's house, the 'sublime sight' of the King's Bench in flames, and the terrible scenes at Langdale's distilleries, says at this point: 'From the instant that the three Bridges over the Thames were occupied by regular troops, the danger was at an end. This awful convulsion, which, on Wednesday, the *seventh* of June, seemed to menace the destruction of everything; was so completed quelled, and so suddenly extinguished, that on the *eighth*, hardly a spark survived of the popular effervescence. Some few persons in the Borough of Southwark,[1] attempted to repeat the outrages of Wednesday; but they were easily and immediately quelled by the military force. Never was a contrast exhibited more striking,

---

[1] *Thrale's Brewery* in Deadman's Place, Southwark, was naturally visited. But here, on the first occasion, 'the clamorous crowd is hush'd by mugs of mum.' Judiciously exhibiting some £50 worth of meat and drink, Mr. Perkins, the Superintendent, contrived to send them away. When they returned they were confronted by soldiers (Hill's 'Boswell's Life of Johnson,' 1887, iii, 435).

than between those two evenings, in the same
city![1] The patroles of Cavalry, stationed in the
Squares and great streets throughout the West
End of the Town, gave London the aspect of a
Garrison; while the Camp which was immediately
afterwards formed in St. James's Park, afforded a
picturesque landscape; both sides of the Canal,
from the Queen's House [*i.e.* Buckingham House]
down to the vicinity of the Horse Guards, being
covered with tents and troops.'[2]

'This audacious tumult is perfectly quelled,'
wrote Gibbon to his stepmother on the 10th.
On the 27th he writes again: 'The measures
of Government have been seasonable and vigorous [!]; and even opposition has been forced to
confess, that the military force was applied and

[1] This is confirmed by Mr. Urban's chronicler: 'The
writer of this paragraph, whose residence is at a small but
equal distance from three dreadful fires which at the same
period were blazing on the Wednesday night, when he
was surrounded by hundreds of families who were dis-
tractedly employed in removing their children and their
valuables, sat down to his literary amusements on Thursday night as uninterruptedly as if he had resided on
Salisbury Plain. Not a human voice was to be heard!'
('Gentleman's Magazine,' August 1780, p. 369.)

[2] Wraxall's 'Historical Memoirs of my Own Time,'
1904, p. 207.

regulated with the utmost propriety. Our danger is at an end, but our disgrace will be lasting, and the month of June 1780, will ever be marked by a dark and diabolical fanaticism, which I had supposed to be extinct, but which actually subsists in Great Britain, perhaps beyond any other Country in Europe.' [1]

Meanwhile, on 9 June, the President of the London Protestant Association, to whose ill-starred plan for placing his Petition before Parliament these deplorable scenes were the calamitous sequel, had been arrested at his house in Welbeck Street, examined by a Committee at the War Office, and escorted to the Tower in charge of an exceptionally strong military guard. He had —it was alleged by his friends—taken no active part in the riots; he had even gone fruitlessly to Buckingham House to offer King George his assistance in checking them, and it was afterwards testified by Sir James Lowther, in whose carriage Lord George had left the house of Commons on the 6th, that he had earnestly entreated the mob to go home and be quiet. Whilst confined in the Tower, he was well supplied with books; and is reported to have devoted himself, among other things, to the study of the ten folio volumes of

[1] Gibbon's 'Corr.,' 1896, i, 382.

the State Trials. According to Malone[1] he applied for 'a Protestant clergyman, a Popish priest, a Presbyterian preacher, and an Anabaptist to be sent to him: but his wishes were not complied with. He then requested to have a fiddler, which was readily granted.' But he was certainly visited, with Lord Stormont's permission, by John Wesley, who, on 19 December spent an hour with him, conversing about Popery and religion. Wesley found him well acquainted with the Bible; and was agreeably surprised to note that he did not complain of any person or thing.[2] After being imprisoned for eight months, on 5 February 1781 he was tried in the Court of King's Bench on a charge of High Treason. His senior counsel was Lloyd (afterwards Lord) Kenyon; the junior, Thomas, later Lord Erskine, then a young man of thirty-one. Lord Mansfield, the aged Lord Chief Justice, presided. The Crown brought witnesses to show that the riots had been the preconcerted results of the demonstration connected with the presentation of the petition; and that Gordon, as the prime mover of that demonstration, was guilty of treason, or—

[1] Charlemont 'Corr.,' Hist. MSS. Comm., 1891, i, 374.

[2] 'Wesley's Journal,' 1901, iv, 185.

to speak precisely—of what was then legally
known as *constructive* treason, that is, something
'equivalent to treason, though not intended or
realized as such.' In this connection, special
stress was laid on the fact that he had signed a
protection by which a house in Long Acre was
saved from destruction. But Kenyon's merciless
cross-examination of the witnesses, particularly of
one William Hay, made havoc of some of the
evidence for the prosecution, while Erskine, in a
concluding speech occupying some sixty octavo
pages of print, and marked by extraordinary
forensic ability, addressed the jury on behalf of
the prisoner. His main contention was that
those petitioners of 2 June, who belonged to the
Protestant Association, had been orderly and
peaceable in their intentions; that his client had
neither part nor lot in the excesses that ensued—
excesses that were 'at the very worst, unforeseen,
undesigned, unabetted and deeply regretted consequences'; and that, in the meaning of the
statute, Gordon was in no wise guilty. These
arguments, admirably marshalled and supported,
must have had their weight with the jury, who,
at a quarter after five o'clock on the morning of
6 February, returned a verdict of 'Not Guilty'—
a verdict which, according to Erskine's editor,

James Ridgway, was 'repeated from mouth to mouth to the uttermost extremities of London, by the multitudes which filled the streets.' Dr. Johnson's comment on the finding, as recorded by Boswell, is characteristic: ' He said he was glad Lord George Gordon had escaped, rather than that a precedent should be established for hanging a man for *constructive treason.*' [1]

' Escaped '—it will be observed—is Johnson's word; and there can be no question that Gordon owed much to the able advocacy of Erskine, who, by the way, besides being a compatriot of his own age, had also begun life as a midshipman. But the precise amount of Lord George's responsibility for the riots is extremely difficult to establish.[2] By his contemporary apologists it is urged that his notification of 29 May had the misfortune to attract in the train of the guileless Protestant Association a host of disreputable auxiliaries,

[1] Hill's ' Boswell's Johnson,' 1887, iv, 87.
[2] Dr. F. A. Wendeborn, Pastor of the German Church on Ludgate Hill, and a witness of the riots, says : ' Lord George Gordon himself, I am convinced, when he began to assemble the mob, never dreamt that matters would be carried to such a height.' He also held that ' no premeditated plan was previously formed by the rioters ' (' View of England towards the Close of the XVIIIth Century,' 1791, ii, 454).

'thieves, pick-pockets, house-breakers' and the like, to whom the 'No Popery' cry meant nothing but a call to disorder; and who were, in fact, an unsolicited and unwelcome contingent from that large, dangerous, and powerful body, the Mob, which, eight and twenty years before, Henry Fielding had ironically termed the real Fourth Estate. They feared, he said, two orders of men only: the justices of the peace and the soldiery—both of which preservers of public tranquillity had, in the occurrences of June 1780, owing to the inactivity of the authorities, for some time left them a free hand. Beginning, for form's sake, with the burning of Popish chapels, impunity had rapidly hurried them on to the destruction of private property, the demolition of public institutions, and to spoliation generally. All this *may* be true. At the same time it is impossible to hold with the 'Gentleman's Magazine,' that the Protestant Association of Coachmakers' Hall were merely 'a set of well-meaning men (*who could not have been aware of the consequences*) [1] met for the defence of the established religion.' The 'consequences' in Scotland had been riots and the burning of Popish chapels; and these were precisely the consequences in

[1] The italics are the writer's.

England, aggravated by special social conditions, and assuredly not modified by the stimulating speeches and reckless rhetoric of Gordon himself, who must have been simplicity personified if he did not know that preaching constitutional restraint to an excitable audience is the idlest of injunctions. To kindle dangerously combustible material is clearly a serious crime, which cannot be condoned on the flimsy pretence that you did not afterwards feed the fire. Yet it was mainly on this latter plea that Gordon was acquitted.

By the historians he has been treated no better than by Horace Walpole. He is a ' crack-brained member of parliament,' a ' half-crazy fanatic,' and so forth. John Forster, who was a Commissioner of Lunacy, regarded him as a madman; and thought those pages of ' Barnaby Rudge ' in which he appeared were the feeblest parts of the book. Dickens, on the contrary, found redeeming points in his ' Protestant hero.' He must, he contended, ' have been at heart a kind man, and a lover of the despised and rejected, after his own fashion. He lived upon a small income, and always within it; was known to relieve the necessities of many people. . . . He always spoke on the people's side, and tried against his muddled brains to expose the profligacy of both parties.

M

He never got anything by his madness, and never sought it.'[1] To this may be added that he was certainly fearless; that he must have possessed considerable persuasive powers as a platform speaker, and that, having gone through the rude discipline of the six years' probation of bad air, bad food, and bad manners, which characterized the orlop deck of a Georgian man-of-war, he could scarcely have emerged without some experimental knowledge of humanity in the rough.

Unfortunately, the remaining incidents of his career enforce rather than extenuate the debatable aspect of his personality. In 1784 we find him girt with a Highland broadsword, donning a Dutch uniform, and inciting the British Seaman, with whom, as an ex-lieutenant, he had naturally a certain authority, to take up arms for the Dutch against the Emperor Joseph. Two years later he is championing the cause of another 'friend of mankind,' Carlyle's 'Sicilian jail-bird,' Cagliostro; and libelling Marie Antoinette for 'publicly persecuting' that egregious impostor. Then he is accused of libelling British justice, in a bogus 'Prisoners' Petition' against transportation, addressed to, but composed by, himself. For these latter exploits, in 1787-8, he was tried and

[1] Forster's 'Life of Dickens,' bk. ii, ch. ix.

eventually sentenced to five years' confinement in Newgate. Already he had become a convert to Judaism—gaberdine and long beard included. In Newgate he lived on the whole not unagreeably, occupying apartments on the Master's side; playing the bagpipes; entertaining friends and admirers daily; giving fortnightly balls, and between whiles, vainly petitioning the French National Assembly to intervene for his release. At the expiration of his sentence, failing to find securities for his good behaviour, he remained in custody, dying at length of jail-fever on the 1st of November 1793 in his forty-second year. 'The Convention have lost a good friend,' was Horace Walpole's comment. His last act was to sing the revolutionary 'Carillon National' of 'Ça ira.' Being refused Jewish burial, he was privately interred in the graveyard of St. James's Chapel in the Hampstead Road. No stone marks the spot.

THE EARLY YEARS OF
MADAME ROYALE

IN the crowded literature arising out of the first
French Revolution, Marie-Thérèse-Charlotte
de France, otherwise Madame Royale, afterwards
Duchesse d'Angoulême, and known to the popular
historian as ' the Orphan of the Temple '—has
certainly not been neglected. Nor, even now,
does the interest in her chequered and sorrowful
story appear to be exhausted. As recently as 1907,
in a volume entitled 'La Fille de Louis XVI,'
the tireless M. George Lenôtre issued a number
of hitherto unpublished papers relating to her
early life, including a reprint, from the text of
the Marquis Costa de Beauregard, of the original
record which she herself drew up in October
1795, before she quitted the Temple—a document which had previously been given to the
world from a transcript only. Two years later,
in 1909, came the ' Madame Duchesse d'Angoulême,' of M. Joseph Turquan, a work which has
the advantage of covering her entire career. And

164

not very long ago appeared at Paris two volumes which also substantially add to our knowledge, one being 'Les Fiançailles de Madame Royale, Fille de Louis XVI, et la première Année de son Séjour à Vienne,' by M. le Comte de Pimodan, a careful and sympathetic study based on fresh material preserved in the Imperial and Royal Archives of Vienna; the other, 'Madame Royale: Sa Jeunesse et son Mariage,' from the persuasive pen of M. Ernest Daudet.[1] The moment is therefore opportune for some brief survey of the subject as disclosed to the most modern research.

Madame Royale, the first child and only daughter of Louis XVI and Marie Antoinette, was born at Versailles on the 19th of December 1778. The tradition of her earlier years, doubtless coloured by the circumstances of her after experiences, represents her as, even in her girlhood, already unusually sedate, very reserved, and abnormally alive to her high position as the descendant of Louis le Grand and the Empress Maria-Theresa. To these characteristics was presently added a growing air of sadness ('la

[1] Since this paper first appeared in February 1913, a translation of M. Daudet's book by Mrs. Rodolph Stawell has been issued by Mr. Heinemann.

petite Madame est triste,' says a contemporary),
which was not likely to decrease as time went
on. Almost from her birth, the air was filled
with disquieting premonitions of the forthcoming
upheaval. In 1789 came the fall of the Bastille.
She was then eleven. On the night of the subsequent 6th October, she was roused suddenly
to see her mother escaping half-dressed from the
furious Femmes de la Halle, who slashed the
vacant bed to tatters. With her parents and her
brother, she made that humiliating progress from
Versailles to Paris, in which the royal carriage
was preceded by the pike-borne heads of murdered
bodyguards. She took part in the momentous but
ill-managed flight to Varennes of June 1791: she
was a witness of the attack of the 20th of June
1792 on the Tuileries, and of the terrible scenes
in August following. Clinging to the Princess
Elizabeth, and with the Dauphin on the other
side listlessly kicking the dead autumn leaves,
she walked in the mournful procession which
made its way across the Tuileries gardens when
the King sought unblessed sanctuary with the
Legislative Assembly. Then came the long,
stifling sojourn in the reporters' box of the
Logographe, and the subsequent transfer of the
party to the tender mercies of the Paris Com-

mune. 'How old is Mademoiselle?' a National guard had asked Marie Antoinette a few days before; and the Queen had answered, 'She is of an age when such scenes are only too horrible!' As a matter of fact, she was not yet fourteen.

It was on Monday, the 13th of August 1792, that the royal family of France entered the prison of the Temple; and in December 1795, more than three years later, Madame Royale was the sole survivor of the group. Her father, her mother, her aunt Elizabeth, had all perished on the scaffold, and her brother, the Dauphin (Louis XVII) was dead.[1] Of the King's fate she had

[1] Here we follow the official accounts. The 'Question Louis XVII' is too large to be discussed in one note—or in many notes. But those who desire to trace to its latest stage the newest petition of the Naundorffs, will do well to consult 'L'Affaire Naundorff: Le Rapport de M. Boissy d'Anglas, Sénateur, commenté et réfuté,' by François Laurentie, Émile Paul, 1911, together with the communications of 'Le Petit Homme Rouge' (Mr. E. A. Vizetelly) to the 'Academy.' It should be added that M. de Pimodan, referring to the Dauphin's death, says expressly that he 'has never found' in the Viennese archives 'the smallest document relating in any way to the pretended survival of Louis XVII' (p. 2, n. 1). [Since this note was written the *legal* right of the Naundorffs to the surname 'de Bourbon' has been confirmed by a French court ('Notes and Queries,' 7 February 1914).]

heard vaguely by the hoarse cries of the newsmen outside the Temple; but it was not until after the Dauphin's death on 8 June 1795 that she became acquainted with the full extent of her losses. Writing in 1796, shortly after she reached Vienna, to her uncle Louis XVIII, then in exile at Blankenburg in Brunswick, she says:

'You have no idea of the hardness of our prison. . . . I myself, who have suffered so much from it, find it almost difficult to believe. My mother was ignorant of the existence of my brother who was lodged underneath her. My aunt and I knew nothing of the transfer of my mother to the Conciergerie, and of her subsequent death. I did not learn it until '95. My aunt was torn from me to be led to the scaffold. In vain I asked why we were separated. The door was shut and bolted without reply. My brother died in the room below me; I was equally uninformed. Finally I did not learn the merited fate of Robespierre, who has made such a noise in the world, until a year after. . . . One can form no idea of the cruelty of those people. But it must be admitted, my dear uncle, that after the death of this monster, my brother and I were better treated. We were given what was necessary, but without telling us what was hap-

pening, and not until after the death of my
brother, did I learn all the horrors and cruelties
committed during those three years.'[1]

Nor is it necessary to recapitulate them now,
especially since, for our present purpose, they are
already sufficiently familiar in the well-known
records of the two valets, Hue and Cléry,[2] and in
the 'Memoir' drawn up in October 1795, by
Madame Royale herself. After the departure of
the Princess Elizabeth from the Temple on the
9th of May 1794 and during the period which
elapsed before the death of Robespierre on the
28th of July following, Madame Royale remained
under the same inexorable surveillance and in a
solitude to which the greatest criminals were
not then subjected. Once Robespierre appeared
abruptly, looked at her insolently, but said nothing. Municipal officers, often drunk, inspected
her daily, spoke to her roughly, refused all information, and took little notice of her requests.
Even after the Terror, when, in consequence of
the visit of Robespierre's victorious adversary,
Barras, somewhat gentler guardians were placed
over her, the strictest silence was remorselessly

[1] Daudet, pp. 18-19.
[2] See 'Cléry's Journal' ('Old Kensington Palace, etc.,'
1910, pp. 238-270).

maintained. There seemed to be no hope of release.

With the death of Louis XVII in June 1795, however, the prospect suddenly brightened; and she was surprised on the 15th of that month by the unexpected entry into her room of Madame Hillaire Chanterenne, a young married woman of thirty, who had been appointed by the ' Comité de Sûreté Générale ' to act as her companion. The delight of the Princess may be imagined. The newcomer was prepossessing, sympathetic and well-informed, and a close friendship speedily sprang up. Madame Chanterenne had been cautioned to be reticent as to the fates of the royal family, the boy-king in particular; but the counsel cannot have been rigidly observed, as in September she told Madame de Tourzel that Madame Royale was ' instruite de tous ses malheurs ';[1] and we know from the Princess herself that she was made acquainted with many things after the death of Louis XVII. Subsequently to the advent of ' sa chère Renète,' as her new friend came soon to be called, she was permitted to receive other visitors: Hue, once the King's valet; her old governess, Madame de Tourzel, and the under-governess, Madame de Mackau.

[1] Lenôtre, ' La Fille de Louis XVI,' 1907, p. 67.

Meanwhile negotiations for her release were slowly proceeding. It has been usually supposed that these originated with Marie Antoinette's nephew, Francis II, Emperor of Germany. But although the question of exchanging French prisoners for the royal family was not a new one, there had been no revival of it at this date, and the immediate cause of the movement which began in June 1795—coupled of course with the weariness of bloodshed which was coming over the community in general—was a memorial addressed to the Convention by the town of Orleans praying for the release and restoration to her relatives of 'cette jeune innocente,' Marie-Thérèse-Charlotte de Bourbon. The result of this appeal was a vote of the Convention on the 30th of June that Madame Royale should be handed over to Austria in exchange for four Conventionists given up to the Austrians by Dumouriez, and for certain other French prisoners.[1] In accordance with these arrangements, Madame Royale quitted the Temple on the 18th-19th of December. She had desired that she might be accompanied by Madame

[1] One of these was Carlyle's 'Old Dragoon' Drouet, who had arrested Louis XVI at Varennes, and who had subsequently become a member of the Convention for the department of la Marne.

Chanterenne; but it had been stipulated on the Austrian side, that she should bring to Vienna no woman who had been domiciled with her at the Temple. She had therefore fallen back on Madame de Mackau's daughter, the Marquise de Soucy. Another attendant was M. Hue, already mentioned, and there were three servants. She was in charge of a captain of gendarmes, named Méchin, and she travelled under the name of 'Sophie.' On the 26th, near Basle, Méchin transferred her to a scrupulous Austrian Polonius, the Prince de Gavre,[1] whose instructions were to conduct her to the capital 'dans les bornes prescrites de l'incognito,' a protection which was not precisely armour of proof, as she was frequently recognized on the road, as indeed she had also been on her way to Basle. At Füssen, in Swabia, on the 30th, she was welcomed by her great-uncle, Prince Clement of Saxony and his sister Cunégonde, the brother and sister of the mother of Louis XVI, who found her 'as interesting as possible.' A few days later, at Innsbrück, she was greeted by one of her mother's sisters, the

---

[1] That delightful little master and picture-chronicler of the Revolution, Duplessi-Bertaux, has left a representation of this scene, which is copied at p. 26 of M. Daudet's book.

Archduchess Elizabeth, Abbess of the Chapter of
the town, who promised to say a daily *Pater* on
her behalf, and assured her that she would be
happy with her Austrian relatives. At Innsbrück
an already-current report seems to have gained
ground that she was to be married off-hand to the
Archduke Charles, a brilliant younger brother of
the Emperor. On the 9th of January she reached
Vienna. Madame de Soucy, by no means the
most discreet of women, was not suffered to remain with her, a perhaps not unreasonable decision, seeing that Austria and the Republic were
at war; and her place was taken by the Countess
Josépha de Chanclos, a distinguished Austrian
lady who had been 'grande maîtresse' to the
Emperor's eldest daughter. Hue, more inoffensive
or more circumspect, was allowed to stay in
Vienna.

Madame Royale's life in the imperial palace
was secluded, and in a sense 'surveillée.' For
this there was the obvious pretext of her period
of mourning, and no doubt also the necessity for
ascertaining to what extent the horrors of her
captivity, graphic details of which had been freely
circulated in France during the last months of
her detention,[1] had affected her health and char-

---

[1] Pimodan, pp. 6-7.

acter. But the question of her marriage came
early to the front. In a letter of August from
Queen Caroline of Naples to her daughter, the
Empress of Germany, it had been already suggested that the Count d'Artois's eldest son, the Duc
d'Angoulême, or the Prince de Condé's grandson, the Duc d'Enghien, would make a suitable
husband. At Innsbrück, as we have seen, a report
had been circulated that she would not be averse
from marrying the popular Archduke Charles.
Between ' Memoirs ' written long after date, and
letters which were either not sent or not received
(however carefully they may have been copied at
the post office), it is difficult to decide at what
particular moment of time Madame Royale became aware of these proposals for her future, or
when she learned that her father and mother had
once destined her for the Duc d'Angoulême, an
arrangement in which her uncle, now known to
royalists as Louis XVIII, of course heartily con-
curred. In any case, for Madame Royale the
wishes of her parents at once became imperative
commands. In a hitherto unpublished letter to
the Duke's brother, the Duc de Berry, dated
from Vienna on the 22nd of January 1796, she
leaves no doubt as to her sentiments in this matter.
" If Angoulême returns to the army of Condé,

beg him from me to write to me, he ought to remember the wishes of our parents as to him and me, I shall never forget them, and I desire that they should come to pass as soon as possible.'[1] Eight days later, in a letter to Louis XVIII, she is no less explicit:[2]

'Sire, I hope that Your Majesty has by this time received my portrait, it was done very hurriedly, and it is very like; I hope to be able one day to send you a drawing of my own; I work a great deal here; I draw, I read, I go out only to walk, this life pleases me greatly, it is the only one that suits my disposition, I love tranquillity, and to do my duties as I ought; I hate trouble and intrigue, which does not suit my age, I know nothing but to love you and to return to you heartily all that I owe you, and also to thank the Emperor from the bottom of my heart for my liberty and for the way in which he treats me, and on which I can but congratulate myself; all that has been said has not a word of truth, all is known, all explained, the Emperor knows the intention of my parents, and much approves it; never has he had any ideas opposed to yours; he approves everything, but he thinks that now is not the time. . . . Everything that was said at

[1] Pimodan, p. 43.   [2] *Ib.* pp. 44-6.

Innsbrück was nothing but infamous calumnies, and you have well judged by your letter of the 9th;[1] I am very tranquil at present, I confess to you; but pardon, I cannot tell you all to-day, it is Sunday, I must go to church for the benediction, adieu my dear Uncle, be, I pray you, quite at ease, and always love your niece who is entirely devoted to you, and ardently desires to receive your letters.'

In a letter of the 2nd of February following, Hue, writing to the King, tells a similar tale. After regretting circuitously that he is not able to console His Majesty for Madame Royale's failure to join him at Verona, he goes on to say that, in spite of what was said at Innsbrück, all the rumours concerning the marriage of Madame with an Archduke are without foundation. 'The Emperor is goodness itself; His Majesty treats Madame with much friendship. He has given her one of the finest and most agreeable apartments of his palace. The Emperor does not mean

[1] This was a letter in which the King had instructed her to say, if any direct propositions were made to her, that she was engaged to her cousin, the Duc d'Angoulême, by her own wish and the will of the King, her uncle. This letter is printed at pp. 51-3 of M. Daudet's book.

to interfere with Madame's tastes in any way; she consequently enjoys with him all the liberty which befits Her Royal Highness's age and position.' And then the astute ex-valet hints tactfully that it would be well for Louis XVIII to signify to the Emperor that he has been fully advised of these amenities. From the Duke of Berry, then with Condé's army on the Rhine, came a letter saying that his father and brother were in Scotland [at Holyrood]; but assuring her on his own account that the Duke would be delighted to fulfil the 'devoir charmant' of marrying his 'très chère Cousine.' Finally followed an epistle from Louis XVIII, who, as may be anticipated, is entirely satisfied with the turn affairs have taken. But as to the precise moment of the marriage, he was no more able to fix it than the Emperor, as he was awaiting political developments. Such, simply told, is the latest version of a marriage contract which has been made the nodus of so much ingenious speculation; and, as suggested by M. de Pimodan, it is quite conceivable that those concerned did no more than follow the trend of their situation from their respective points of view. Whatever had been in the air, the outcome at all events was, that about a fortnight after Madame Royale's arrival at Vienna

N

she was formally engaged to her cousin, the Duc d'Angoulême.

This matter set definitely at rest, her so-called 'claustration'—if it existed—became less strict. She left off her mourning; began to take part in the entertainments of the Viennese Court, and even appeared with the royal family at the theatre. Whatever may have been the aloofness and austerity charged against her in later years, there were no signs of it now. 'Absolutely all the documents of the epoch,' says M. de Pimodan, 'are unanimous in praising the grace of Madame Royale, her amiability, and the courteous facility of her elocution.' Apart from the burning question of her marriage, her only desire was to join at Rome her aunts, Madame Adélaïde and Madame Victoire, the daughters of Louis XV, and to visit her uncle at Verona on the way. But events conspired to prolong her stay in Austria. Acting on the orders of the recently established French Directory, the Venetian government notified Louis XVIII to vacate its dominions. This led him to take a step which he must have instinctively known would be distasteful to Francis II: he joined the army of the Prince de Condé at Riegel. Although received with enthusiasm by the Royalist troops, Austrian diplomacy could not suffer such a disturbing element to remain in the camp; and he was promptly informed by the cabinet of Vienna that if he did not depart it would be necessary to expel him. Repulsed here and there in different principalities, he found at last a tolerated resting-place at Blankenburg in the Duchy of Brunswick, where, for a brief space, 'surrounded by intrigues and uncertainties,' he maintained a miniature court in three rooms hired from a brewer's widow. His wife, meanwhile, was living on sufferance in the Bishopric of Passau in Bavaria. With September 1797 came the 'coup d'état' (18th Fructidor), by which two members of the Directory were proscribed for favouring royalty—a step which made the restoration of the Bourbons farther off than ever; and not long afterwards the Duke of Brunswick was recommended by the King of Prussia to get rid of his inconvenient guest with the least possible delay. So stringent were the orders, that it was impossible to secure even a few days' respite; and in the middle of February 1798, the unfortunate Louis XVIII set out again, this time for Russia —where he had for long been negotiating with Catherine II to obtain an asylum. After her death (17 November 1796) her successor, Paul I, consented to receive him, and on the 23rd of March he took up his abode at Mittau, in Courland.

Meanwhile Madame Royale remained in Vienna. Her residence there has been styled an exile; sometimes an actual imprisonment. Exile from France it certainly amounted to; but in other respects she was, as compared with others of her relatives, in a state of comparative security. With the successes of Bonaparte in Italy, and the subsequent operations of the forces of the Directory in Germany, her marriage, once settled, fell, both with her uncle and Francis II, out of the range of urgent agenda. From her betrothed, lingering vaguely at Holyrood with his father, in the hope of joining in some expedition against France, she received occasional letters. But he was not a demonstrative person, and though respectful and affectionate, those of his communications which have been printed can scarcely be said to palpitate with passion. As time went on, there are indications that, owing to Madame Royale's being continually forced by circumstances into the rôle of apologist or petitioner to the Emperor for one or other member of her scattered family, her position at the Viennese court became one of considerable difficulty.

She heartily detested intrigue; and both Louis XVIII and his counsellor, d'Avaray, were masters of finesse (to give it the mildest name), while the King, moreover, was a very Micawber of the pen. Now and then, with a touch of decision which her isolated position makes more memorable, she had the courage to resist propositions which did not accord with her principles. Her uncle, having addressed an open letter to the Abbé Edgeworth, the confessor of Louis XVI, was anxious that his niece should draw up a similar epistle, affixing to it the date of her release from the Temple. But apart from the dissatisfaction with which she knew such a document would be regarded by the Emperor, she shrank from the deception of the date. 'I will not conceal from you,' she wrote, 'that I should be sorry to antedate a letter; such a thing may be done by older persons [she does not wish to offend her uncle], and in cases which demand it: but it is part of my age and my character to be as simple and exact as truth.'[1] There can be no doubt that differences of this kind did not tend to lessen the gloom which was gradually succeeding to the first exhilaration of her liberation from captivity. And, in addition to this, there was, at all events

[1] Pimodan, p. 78.

at first, another ever-recurring source of embarrassment and regret. As the sole surviving representative of her family, Madame Royale naturally became the point of resort for all those petitioners whom the collapse of royalty had involved in its fall. Having nothing herself but her German pension, it was out of the question for her to comply with their appeals; and her almoner and intermediary, the Bishop of Nancy, La Fare, then at Vienna, must often have been hard put to it to find fresh forms of expressing the refusals which, however unwillingly, she had no choice but to make.[1]

In 1799, after prolonged negotiations between the King and the Emperors of Russia and Germany, Madame Royale at last quitted Vienna to join Louis XVIII at Mittau, to which place he

[1] Some of the cases were no doubt unreasonable or extortionate, but not a few were tragic. Take, for instance, that of Madame de Korff and her mother, Madame de Stegelmann, who had advanced all their means (262,000 francs) in aid of the equipment of the cumbrous Korff 'berline,' which played so prominent a part in the frustrate flight to Varennes. When, with the captivity in the Temple, the interest on the debt ceased to be paid, the hapless lenders of the money became practically destitute; and it was only by the strictest economy that Madame Royale could render them inadequate assistance.

had summoned his wife, who arrived there on the
2nd of June. On the following day his niece,
with a suite which included the faithful valets
Hue and Cléry, made her appearance. The King
had set off early in the morning. They were to
meet at the first post-house; but the Princess,
travelling faster, reached it before her uncle, and
went farther along the road. As the two carriages neared, the occupants alighted. It was a
meeting of many tears. Louis XVIII had not
seen his niece since June 1791, on the eve of the
flight to Varennes. At that date she was a girl of
thirteen, while the cousin to whom she was now to
be married was but three years older. In spite of her
terrible experiences, she had now grown into a
beautiful young woman, with much of the dignity
and grace of her mother and grandmother; and—
in her clear blue eyes and mournful smile—
something of the saintly Princess Elizabeth. She
was speedily presented to the Queen; to the aged
Abbé Edgeworth, then domiciled at Mittau; and
to the former bodyguard of her father, now in
her uncle's service. But the person who must
naturally have interested her most was her future
husband, whose portrait, painted and written, she
had already received from Louis XVIII. His
qualities apparently were more sound than showy.

If not remarkable for wit or elegance, he is admitted to have been loyal and religious, with great courage and good sense. 'His excellent principles and character cannot but contribute to make me happy'—she wrote sanguinely to the Empress of Germany; but it must be confessed that he was scarcely at the level of his destined bride. Seven days after her arrival at Mittau she married him, the marriage certificate being signed by the Czar, and deposited in the archives of the Russian senate.

At the little court in Courland the influence of the young duchess speedily made itself felt for good. 'To see her,' says a biographer, unconsciously echoing Steele's famous compliment, 'was to be edified.' But it was decreed that her troubles were soon to be renewed. Suddenly, though perhaps not unexpectedly, Paul I, whom circumstances had now brought over to the side of Bonaparte, ordered Louis XVIII to quit Russia forthwith—simultaneously withdrawing his pension. It was the eve of the anniversary of the execution of Louis XVI, and the Duchess with difficulty obtained the two days' seclusion which she usually devoted to her father's memory. On the 22nd of January 1801, she started for Memel with her uncle, her husband being with Condé's army.[1] Accompanied by a few followers they made their way painfully through Lithuania. They were almost penniless; and at Memel the Duchess had to raise money on her diamonds. Eventually, with Bonaparte's concurrence, they obtained leave from the King of Prussia to reside at Warsaw, on condition that Louis XVIII reduced his suite to a minimum, and took the title of the 'Count de Lille.' At Warsaw the Duke, who had distinguished himself as a soldier, rejoined his wife. Then came the assassination of the Czar; and his successor, Alexander, more clement to the exiles, renewing the subsidy, invited them to return to Mittau. This, however, they did not do until December 1804, when Bonaparte's influence with Prussia again obliged them to 'move on.'

The second residence in Courland had no marked incident except the death of the Abbé Edgeworth. After Eylau, many wounded French prisoners arrived in Mittau. Contagious fever

[1] A contemporary print, circulated clandestinely in Paris, shows her travelling on foot with her uncle through a snowclad landscape escorted by an inquisitive poodle, perhaps her dog, Coco. In another, she is called the 'French Antigone'—Antigone being the name which 'classic Louis' himself applied to her in a letter to the Prince de Condé.

broke out among them; and Edgeworth at once went to their assistance, only to succumb himself. He was nursed by the Duchess, who, regardless of her own risk, refused all aid; but he died in May 1807. A few months later, although Alexander refrained from openly harassing his guest, it became evident that looking to his relations with Bonaparte, residence in Russia was no longer practicable, and Louis XVIII consequently resumed his wanderings. In October he embarked at Riga for Sweden, where Gustavus IV placed a frigate at his disposal. In this he sailed for England. He was uninvited, and consequently not very welcome. The British Government were tired of the plotting of the refugees, and on reaching Yarmouth he was officially informed that he must go to Holyrood. This, however, he firmly declined to do; and eventually, with Pitt's goodwill, an interim retreat was found for him at Gosfield Hall in Essex, an old Tudor mansion which had come to the first Marquess of Buckingham with his wife, Mary Nugent, the daughter of the Lord Clare to whom Goldsmith addressed the poem of the 'Haunch of Venison.' It was a roomy building with a fine lake and park, in which latter the grateful exiles erected a votive temple to their host. This they encircled with five oaks, the first

HARTWELL HOUSE, BUCKS.

(FROM N. WHITTOCK'S DRAWING, ENGRAVED BY HIMSELF)

planted by the 'Count de Lille,' the second by
his wife, the third by his niece, and the others
by his two nephews, the Dukes of Angoulême
and Berry, all of whom were now gathered on
these hospitable shores.

In April 1809, the little colony, mainly with a
view to get nearer London, moved to Hartwell
House in Bucks, two miles from Aylesbury, on
the right hand of the road to Thame. This they
hired from the owner, the Rev. Sir George Lee,
Bart., for an annual rental of £500. Although
Hartwell was spacious enough to be described as
a place 'wherein misery might be tolerably comfortable on £24,000 a year,'[1] the accommodation
was necessarily inadequate for an establishment
of some 140 persons, which occasionally increased
to 200. The great pannelled rooms with the
carved ceilings had consequently to be subdivided;
and sheds were erected in the grounds for the
servants. Even the 'Count de Lille's' own private
apartment shrank to a mere ship's cabin. But
in these contracted conditions the formalities of
Court life which had existed at Blankenburg and

---

[1] The allowance from the British Government was reported to be £20,000, namely £14,000 for the King, and
£6,000 for the Duc d'Angoulême (Smyth's 'Aedes Hart-
wellianae,' 1851, p. 391).

Mittau were minutely maintained. The flag with the 'fleurs de lis'[1] still floated from the house-top. Dukes figured as Captains of an undiscoverable Body-guard or Gentlemen of an exiguous Bed-chamber. The 'Count de Lille'—simple 'particulier' though he professed to be—still made imposing migration from the drawing-room to the dining-room, and back to the drawing-room again, his niece curtseying profoundly at his exits and entrances, while he as punctiliously kissed her hand. When, on rare occasions, he came to town to attend a French place of worship, it was with all the accompaniments of quasi-royal state.

In the unpromising outlook on the Continent, these things had, however, become, if not a mockery, little more than a memory, and return to France a consummation no longer to be dreamed of. Politics, indeed, had ceased as a theme of

---

[1] This is said to be still preserved at Hartwell House, where portraits of Louis XVIII and the Prince de Condé hang in the Queen's room. Elsewhere is the King's 'prie-Dieu.' The apartments of the Duke and Duchess of Angoulême were at the south-west angle of the building. Under two worn stones in Hartwell Churchyard lie Field-Marshal the Count de la Chapelle and the Queen's first physician, the Chevalier Collignon, both of whom died during the Hartwell occupation.

conversation, which fell back on 'belles-lettres,'[1] history and languages, largely supplemented by the long stories of the master of the house, who had now reached the age when youthful recollections assume the proportions of Canterbury Tales.[2] Something of animation was imported into this 'set, gray life,' by the vivacity of two

[1] 'Louis Dixhuit is a universal reader'—says Mrs. Thrale, in her Notes on Boswell; and she adds that he delighted in reading 'Tom Jones' (Hayward's 'Autobiography,' etc., 1861, ii, 129).

[2] Gastronomy was another of his distractions—and translating Horace. To both of these things Byron refers in that 'Age of Bronze' which he wrote at Genoa in 1823:

'Good classic Louis! is it, canst thou say,
Desirable to be the " Désiré?"
Why wouldst thou leave calm Hartwell's green abode,
Apician table, and Horatian ode,
To rule a people who will not be ruled,
And love much rather to be scourged than school'd?'

He goes on to call him :

'A mild Epicurean, form'd, at best,
To be a kind host and as good a guest,
To talk of letters, and to know by heart
One *half* the poet's, *all* the gourmand's art :
A scholar always, now and then a wit,
And gentle when digestion may permit
But not to govern lands enslav'd or free;
The gout was martyrdom enough for thee.'

clever women, Madame de Damas and Madame
de Narbonne. But, on the whole, existence at
Hartwell must have been hopelessly monotonous.
Between an adoring but uninteresting husband
and a gouty and garrulous uncle, the Duchess of
Angoulême, naturally serious, and saddened by
circumstance, found her chief occupation in
charity and devotional exercises. In 1810 a
closer attention to Louis XVIII devolved on her
by the death of the Queen, who, after a solemn
Roman Catholic service at the Portman Square
Chapel, was borne with regal honours to Westminster Abbey.[1] Among other valedictory utterances, the poor lady is reported to have exclaimed
to the Duchess, ' As to you, my niece, you only
want wings to carry you to heaven!'

For four years more the ' Count de Lille'
vegetated in his Buckinghamshire asylum. Then
came Leipzig, the fall of Bonaparte, and the surrender of Paris to the Allies. The Dukes of
Angoulême and Berry hurriedly left England to
favour, as they might, the royalist cause; and
shortly afterwards (25 March 1814), carriages
with white cockades came dashing up the Hart-

[1] Her remains were shortly afterwards transferred to
the crypt of the Cathedral at Cagliari. She was the
daughter of the King of Sardinia.

well avenue containing a deputation from Bordeaux to announce the Restoration of the Bourbons. Close upon this, followed official congratulations from the Prince Regent; and in the middle of the night the King, at last ' de facto,' roused his niece to tell her the good news.

His progress to London shortly afterwards was triumphal. At Stanmore the Prince Regent came to meet him with an equipage adorned not only with white cockades but with postilions in white coats and waistcoats. Over part of the route the new monarch's vehicle was drawn by the excited populace, who took the horses from the shafts. Hyde Park and Piccadilly were thronged by enthusiasts; and it was not until seven o'clock that the King reached Grillion's Hotel, in Albemarle Street,[1] where he was to put up. The grateful speech which he made to the Prince Regent has been blamed by French critics, who hold that His Majesty gave far too much credit to the part played by England in the Restoration. But his welcome in London had surely been such as might turn any one's head. A magnificent

---

[1] Grillion's Hotel—probably by some pre-occupation with 'premier capitaine du monde' of Henri IV—is generally spoken of by Madame Royale's French biographers as ' l'hôtel Crillon.'

fête, 'dazzling with lights and gilding,' was given in the gallery at Carlton House. 'Nothing,' says one who was present, 'could be finer. . . .' 'The Prince had invited not only the Princes and Princesses of England, but had taken particular care to collect about the King the faithful "émigrés," those illustrious names of France, who had afforded a distinguished example of self-devotion.'[1]   Louis XVIII also held a reception himself at Grillion's, Madame D'Arblay, as the wife of a French General Officer, being among those presented. She was greeted, according to her own account, with the utmost condescension, saluted as 'Madame la Comtesse,' and highly complimented on her works.[2]   On the 24th of April the King left Dover in the 'Royal Sovereign' yacht for Calais, accompanied of course by his niece. On the 3rd of May the Baron de Frénilly witnessed their grand entry into Paris by the Faubourg St. Denis in a calash with eight horses, Louis XVIII wearing a blue overcoat with gold epaulettes and an enormous three-cornered hat.

[1] 'Memoirs of the Duchesse de Gontaut,' Davis' trans., 1894, i, 145.

[2] 'Diary, etc. of Madame D'Arblay,' 1905, vi, pp. 117, 133. She missed presentation to the Duchess, whom she saw afterwards at the Tuileries in February 1815.

He had celebrated his accession by a fit of the gout, seemed sadly tired, and was apparently insensible to the shouts of joy that filled the air as he passed.[1] 'The Duchesse d'Angoulême was much more the object of public enthusiasm; but she looked stiff and unnatural in a new corset, and her naturally sad face recalled either the past or predicted the future.'[2]

Here—following the example of the books on which we have most depended—we pause. M. de Pimodan stops at the betrothal; M. Daudet, at the marriage; M. Lenôtre, at Vienna. To stretch the narrative a little farther, we have included the English residence, which closes with the first Restoration. But after this Madame Royale had nearly forty years to live before she died, a child-less widow, at Frohsdorf in Austria, on the 13th of October 1851. Her exiles had by no means finished at Hartwell; and her life had

---

[1] He was by this time exceedingly stout—so stout indeed, that the portrait-painters of the day dared not draw him accurately lest they should be accused by the police of caricature. ('Early Married Life of Maria Josepha, Lady Stanley,' 1900, 2nd edn., p. 385, where the Duchess is described as 'thin, genteel, grave and dignified.')

[2] 'Memoirs of the Baron de Frénilly,' Lees' trans., 1909, 251.

O

been full of bitter disappointments. There seems to be agreement that, as time went on, her character hardened—that she lost something of that forgiving spirit which had prompted her, as a girl, to write on her prison-wall at the Temple: 'Mon Dieu, pardonnez à ceux qui ont fait périr mes parents.' Certain it is, that her early sufferings gradually came to brood like a hateful nightmare on her later life. Every recollection brought with it a shudder of indescribable horror; and a passionate desire to blot out for ever the details of her past experiences. Nevertheless, she remains a great personality, who only required a fitting environment for fitting expansion. She was a wonderful mixture of subdued natural sensibility and cultivated moral strength. Under trial she showed extraordinary equanimity; in moments of emergency, unexpected decision. Piety, pride of race, a love of country, an undeviating sense of duty—all helped to mould her disposition. She had, one would think, some of the austerer qualities of the Spanish saint who was her namesake. Both by her virtues and her misfortunes she stands at a far higher altitude than the smaller souls about her; and that adroit aphorist, Bonaparte, was not far out when he described her as 'the only man of her family.'

A LITERARY PRINTER

WRITING in May 1792 to Lord Sheffield, Mr. Edward Gibbon, then ' of Lausanne,' appears to have been unusually disturbed by the absence of certain information he had been expecting from London. In the 'Gentleman's Magazine' for August 1788—which only reached him in his Swiss retirement long after date—had appeared ' a very curious and civil account of the Gibbon family'; and he desired to correspond with the writer, whose personality was disguised by the initials 'N.S.,' standing possibly for ' no signature.' To this end, he had, in the previous February, addressed a courteous communication to the proprietor of the magazine; but up to the time of his letter to Lord Sheffield had not received any reply. He therefore begged his friend to ' call upon Mr. John Nichols, bookseller and printer, at Cicero's Head, Red-Lion-passage, Fleet-street, and ask him whether he did not, about the beginning of March, receive a very polite letter from Mr. Gibbon of Lausanne?'

adding—though not as part of the message—
' To which, either as a man of business or a civil
Gentleman, he should have returned an answer.'
Lord Sheffield cannot have acted very promptly
on this commission, for it is renewed three months
later, and repeated to Gibbon's publisher, Cadell.
However, by October, Nichols had apparently
shown signs of vitality; and all was well ' in the
best of possible worlds.'   The writer of the article
eventually turned out to be that eccentric baronet
and genealogist, Egerton Brydges, whose grandmother was a Gibbon, and who, many years later,
published a letter which the historian addressed
to him on this very subject.[1]

But Brydges never saw his new-found relative,
for Gibbon, shortly after his return to England,
died at his St. James's Street lodgings; and in
the ' Gentleman's Magazine ' for January 1794,
Nichols, then managing that periodical, forthwith
printed the ' very polite letter ' mentioned above.
It is notable—in addition to its main purpose—
for two things: one being Gibbon's magniloquent
characterization of Nichols as ' the last, or one of
the last, of the learned Printers '; the other, its
suggestion that the interesting literary, historical,

[1] ' Autobiography of Sir Egerton Brydges, Bart.,' 1834,
i, 225.

and miscellaneous papers dispersed through ' Mr. Urban's ' pages should be withdrawn from their more ephemeral context, classified carefully, and re-issued as a separate publication of moderate size.[1] Something of this Nichols had already done for the 'Memoirs' of his master, Bowyer ; something more he did by expanding that work into the invaluable ' Literary Anecdotes and Illustrations of the Eighteenth Century.' These compilations, it is not too much to say, are as indispensable to the students of the period they embrace as the D.N.B. or 'Notes and Queries' would now be to anyone engaged on the history of the last century. How far Nichols was encouraged in his enterprise by Gibbon's hint, upon which he did not act directly, must be matter of conjecture. But in his several capacities of Printer, Antiquary, Editor and Writer, he was long a prominent personality ; and, backed by the commendation of the author of the ' Decline and Fall '—even if one does not rate that certificate as highly as the author of ' Vanity Fair ' rated

---

[1] John Walker's 'Selection of Curious Articles from the Gentleman's Magazine,' third ed., 1814, 4 vols., partly complies with this proposal. In our day the exhaustive ' Gentleman's Magazine Library,' edited by Sir Laurence Gomme (1883-1906), covers wider ground.

it [1]—may fairly claim to deserve some passing record.

Like Laureate Whitehead, Nichols was the son of a baker. He was born on the 2nd of February in the eventful '45, at Islington, then a pleasant village detached from London, where there were still green lanes and lingering traces of woodland; and where, from Elizabeth's old hunting lodge of Canonbury Tower, the amateur of altitudes could (as per advertisement) enjoy a ' Prospect into five Counties' at once. His school days were spent in the local academy of John Shield, whose earliest scholar was William Hawes, later the founder of the Royal Humane Society, but more memorable to letters as the Strand apothecary who ministered to Goldsmith in his last illness. For eight years Nichols was his instructor's favourite pupil; and he was at first intended for the Navy. But the death, in 1751, of Lieutenant Wilmot, of the ' Bellona,' a connection from whom much was expected, put an end to this project; and in 1757 the boy was apprenticed to William Bowyer, the younger, a well-known printer in Dockwell Court, Whitefriars. Bowyer, who had been

---

[1] 'To have your name mentioned by Gibbon, is like having it written on the dome of St. Peter's.' (Thackeray's ' English Humourists,' 1858, p. 275.)

educated at St. John's College, Cambridge, was
a man of superior attainments, and seems to have
very thoroughly carried out his obligations as a
master, since, in addition to educating his apprentice as a typographer, he is said to have given him
a very fair classical training. And Nichols had,
moreover, literary inclinations of his own, which,
contrary to all tradition, his employer encouraged.
He scribbled verse for popular anthologies; sang
the praises of his native Islington; and contributed
youthful essays to the 'Westminster Journal'
under the style of ' The Cobbler of Alsatia.'

What caused writers at this date to masquerade
so frequently as 'Cobblers' is not now readily
apparent; [1] but for the locality chosen, there was
ample justification. Bowyer's premises in Dockwell, or Dogwell Court, were situated in the very
heart of that former ' debtors' sanctuary and
thieves' paradise,' the ' Alsatia ' of Scott's ' Fortunes of Nigel.' We have it moreover on Nichols'
own authority that his master's printing-office
had actually been the 'George Tavern' of Thomas

---

[1] Robert Lloyd wrote in the ' St. James's Magazine ' in
1763 as ' The Cobbler of Tissington'; Colman, as ' The
Cobbler of Cripplegate.' Perhaps it is to be connected
with the popularity of James Woodhouse (see p. 41),
who published his ' Poems on Sundry Occasions' in 1764.

Shadwell's 'Squire of Alsatia'; and consequently the favoured rendezvous of its 'Soldadoes and Fooladoes'—its Scrapealls and Cheatlys and Captain Hackums.[1] But with William of Orange the unblessed privileges of the place had passed away; and under the third George but little of 'bombard-phrase,' buff belts, and rusty 'toasting-irons' could have haunted the patient compositors at Whitefriars, peering curiously over the crabbed texts of Buxtorfius and Hedericus. The chief event of these early days, as regards Nichols, was a fruitless mission to Cambridge, on his employer's behalf, to secure the University printing—an office which that learned body, no doubt wisely, elected to retain in its own hands. But his want of success did not diminish his favour with Bowyer; and, young as he was, Nichols was rapidly acquiring a reputation for ability. Already he was a freeman of London, and a Liveryman of the Company of Stationers; and in 1764, when he was twenty, Bowyer took him formally into partnership. Three years later they moved from Dockwell Court, where Bowyer had been born and had lived for nearly sixty-seven years, to

[1] It is now 'part of the establishment' of Messrs. Bradbury, Agnew and Co. ('London Past and Present,' by H. B. Wheatley, 1891, iii, 504).

Gibbon's Red-Lion-passage, on the north side of Fleet Street, a little to the east of Fetter Lane. Over the lintel they set up a bust of Cicero, bearing, in reference to Johann Fust's early editions of ' Tully's Offices,' the inscription— ' M. T. Cicero, a quo primordia preli.'

By this time, however, Bowyer had grown old and infirm. But the unwearied ' Architectus Verborum '—as he styled himself professionally —persisted, almost to the end, in correcting personally the Greek texts he printed; and his last effort was a fresh edition of a work which he had always admired, Bentley's ' Dissertation on the Epistles of Phalaris,' duly equipped and augmented with marginalia collected from Warburton, Lowth, Clarke, and others. This was published in 1777. In the same year Bowyer died; and was buried at Low Leyton in Essex. Nichols, one of his executors, at this date two-and-thirty, came into part of his personal estate, and succeeded to the business. He was a widower; but was soon to marry again. He had also adventured seriously in letters. One of his earliest enterprises was the annotating with Bowyer in 1774 of two Essays on the ' Origin of Printing '; and he had himself edited some supplementary volumes of Swift, besides being responsible for an edition of the

miscellaneous writings in verse and prose of
William King, that jovial and jocular judge of
the Irish High Court of Admiralty who figures
in Johnson's 'Lives' (between Duke and Sprat!)
as the author of an Horatian 'Art of Cookery.'
In both these efforts Nichols had been materially
assisted by Isaac Reed, the Staple Inn solicitor,
one of those enigmatical personages who would
help anyone, but ' rather stand in the pillory than
put his name to a book.' What, however, must
be regarded as Nichols' true beginning was the
' Brief Memoirs of Mr. Bowyer,' a pamphlet of
fifty-two pages which, in 1778, was circulated
privately among a few of his master's old friends.
With this in reality originated the long series
of biographical, bibliographical, and anecdotical
publications mainly associated with his name, and
for which his labours are still in request. In spite
of Gibbon's laudation, he was scarcely, like
Bowyer, a scholar. 'He never (he himself tells
us) affected to possess any superior share of erudition, or to be profoundly versed in the learned
languages; content, if in plain and intelligible
terms, either in conversation or in writing, he
could contribute his quota of information or entertainment.'[1] To this modest estimate should be

[1] ' Literary Anecdotes, etc., 1812, vi, 630.

added that he was untiring in curiosity, and indefatigable in the assembling of material of all sorts.
He had, moreover, the invaluable faculty of attracting into his archaeological and antiquarian
projects a number of amateurs and learned volun-
teers of the Reed type whose activities kept him
continually supplied with relays of gratuitous
information.

One of the first results of the welcome accorded
to the Bowyer sketch of 1778 was a sixpenny
pamphlet, issued in 1781, under the title 'Biographical Anecdotes of William Hogarth; and a
Catalogue of his Works chronologically arranged;
with occasional Remarks.' Hogarth had died as
far back as 1764; but nothing of any critical
importance had been written about him until, in
October 1780, Horace Walpole at last issued his
long-withheld fourth volume of the 'Anecdotes
of Painting,' in which he gave some account of
the artist, as well as a list of his engravings based
chiefly on the Strawberry Hill collection. Walpole's book had the effect of creating what would
now be called a 'boom' in Hogarth prints; and
Nichols—who had contemplated some brief mention of Hogarth in the extended biography of
Bowyer which he had then at press—seized the
opportunity of turning his loose notes into a

separate work, in which task he was largely helped by Reed and others. Foremost of these latter was that peculiarly captious critic, George Steevens, the Shakespeare commentator, who was also a Hogarth collector; and who, from a unique copy of Nichols's pamphlet, which is preserved at the British Museum, seems to have aided his associate by insidiously interpolating, among other things, some exceedingly 'severe reflections' on his Twickenham rival. These, however, were fortunately modified before publication; and, in a subsequent issue of the 'Anecdotes of Painting,' Walpole frankly acknowledged that Nichols's researches were much more accurate and satisfactory than his own, and that they omitted nothing 'a Collector would wish to know; either with regard to the history of the painter himself, or to the circumstances, different editions, and variations of his Prints.' He added, as in duty bound, that he had completed his list of Hogarth's works from Nichols.

This utterance belongs to 1786; and, before that date, Nichols had expanded his slender tract of 1781 into a thick three-shilling book, which by 1785 [1] had grown to more than five hundred

---

[1] The writer possesses the actual copy of the intermediate, or second edition of 1782 prepared by Nichols

pages. Twenty years later (1808-10), and some time after Steevens's death, this had increased once more to two portly quarto volumes, entitled at large: 'The Genuine Works of William Hogarth; illustrated with Biographical Anecdotes, a Chronological Catalogue, and a Commentary,' by John Nichols and the late George Steevens. To these, in 1817, was added a third; and the three volumes constitute the mine from which modern biographical accounts of Hogarth have mainly been quarried. Recent research has rectified minor errors of fact; and fuller knowledge has come to recognize, not too soon, a side of the artist's genius which his contemporaries, hoodwinked by the clamorous picture-dealers and connoisseurs, were content to ignore, namely—

for the edition of 1785. At the beginning is pasted a slip inscribed : 'This Vol. belongs to Mr. Nichols, Printer, Red Lion Passage, Fleet street. G.S. [i.e. George Steevens].' In a note to the 'Literary Anecdotes,' 1812, vi, 632, Nichols admits that he was 'indebted for nearly every critique' on Hogarth's plates to Steevens, who, he adds, wrote the 'Prefaces' to the second and third editions. This is confirmed by the copy above described, in which the introductory 'Memorandum,' although initialed 'J. N. Nov. 10, 1785,' is wholly in Steevens's handwriting— further evidence of which is frequent in the succeeding pages. Steevens also made numerous corrections before his death, with a view to a fresh edition.

his extraordinary merits as a painter; but it is nevertheless from Nichols and Steevens that we derive most of our general information respecting him. And it is clear that a large proportion of this information is directly attributable to Steevens, who, whenever he could restrain his ingrained tendency to malevolent aspersion—a tendency favoured by his ambush of anonymity[1]—was without doubt a highly-instructed interpreter of the 'graphic representations' which Charles Lamb rightly ranked, for their 'teeming, fruitful, suggestive meaning,' rather with books than pictures. In the oft-quoted words: 'Other pictures we look at—his [Hogarth's] prints we read.'

It is excusable to linger on the 'Anecdotes of Hogarth,' because too little importance has hitherto been attached to their position and value in the Nichols bibliography. Usually priority is given to the 'Memoirs of Bowyer,' really published a year later—since the first tentative issue of 1778 cannot be said to have been published at all; and the Hogarth book had its birth and being while the 'Memoirs of Bowyer,' which took four years to print before it appeared in

---

[1] In the 'Genuine Works,' Nichols took the precaution of indicating, by notes or quotation marks, most of his collaborator's more mischievous contributions.

1782, was still on the stocks. Bowyer was undoubtedly a notable man; and perhaps, even
more than his ' apprentice, partner and successor '
(these are Nichols' words on his title-page), deserves the praise of Gibbon as ' the last, or one of
the last, of the learned Printers.' He had, as we
have seen, received a University education, by
which he profited; and at Cambridge he made
many learned friends, who remained his friends
through life. When, in 1722, he became his
father's partner, he at once took charge of the
literary and critical department, almost immediately earning the approbation of that heavily
erudite typographical antiquary, Michael Mait-
taire, for whom he afterwards set up those metrical
'Senilia,' of which Johnson could be persuaded to
say no more than that they made Carteret a
dactyl. Bowyer grew interested in philology and
archaeology; and books bearing his imprint
speedily obtained a definite reputation, equal
only to that of his contemporaries, Baskerville
and the two Foulises. Moreover, he was a close
critic of texts, a commentator, and (like Richardson after him) a diligent compiler of Prefaces,
Indexes, and ' honest Dedications.' To such
works as Wilkins's ' Selden ' and the ' Reliquiæ
Baxterianæ' he rendered substantial aid; he

helped much in the dictionaries of Littleton, Schrevelius, Buxtorf and Hederich; introduced an English version of Montesquieu's 'Grandeur et Décadence des Romains, and was one of the many correctors of Conyers Middleton's 'Cicero.' Numismatology was also among his hobbies; and he supplemented the labours in this direction of his old college friend, William Clarke. His most enduring work was his 'Critical Conjectures on the New Testament'; his last has been already mentioned. He is an excellent example of the old unhasting, unresting craftsman and book-man, laborious, assiduous, conscientious—dying placidly at last, after a long life, with honour and troops of friends. James Basire engraved a capital portrait of him at seventy-eight—a lean, learned face, looking out of a symmetrical cauli-flower wig—with hooked nose, steady eyes, and precise, close-pressed lips. There is also a bust of him in Stationers' Hall.

His career, it is true, was not eventful; and, in his partner's 'Memoirs,' the 'troops of friends' bear about the same proportion to the life-story as the notes of the biographer to the text. Indeed it would require a Mathias or a Warton or an Isaac d'Israeli to defend the extraordinary liberality of the Nichols scheme of annotation. Often a

single line at the head of a quarto page is followed by a note of more than forty lines in small
type, frequently extending over-leaf, and not
seldom annotated in its turn. Now and then the
page is all note. And there is something in the
contention of Walpole, who, commending Nichols
for accuracy, observes that he calls too many people
'great.' ' I have known several of his heroes (says
Horace) who were very *little* men.' Indeed, for
not a few of Bowyer's more illustrious contemporaries—for Goldsmith, for Gray, for Smollett, for Sterne—one must be content to seek in
vain. You may look for them, as, in the ' Citizen
of the World,' Lien-Chi-Altangi looked for the
' sommités littéraires ': they are not distinguish-
able, because they are not present. Richardson,
a brother-printer, has, to be sure, a longish passage, obscurely assigned, for its main substance,
to ' the writer of the verses annexed to the fourth
edition of " Clarissa." ' It contains little but
what are now familiar facts, of which the only
one relevant is, that Bowyer printed the first
volume of the Abbé Prévost's paraphrase of
' Pamela.' A second note deals at length with
the iniquitous doings of Messieurs Exshaw,
Wilson, and Saunders, the ' Irish Rapparees ' who
' invaded ' Richardson's property by piratically

P

anticipating the authorized publication at Dublin of 'Sir Charles Grandison.' Hogarth, who, we know, had already been withdrawn from Nichols' pages for special and separate treatment, figures only in a note to Dr. Trusler's moralizing of him, which Bowyer printed. Fielding is mentioned, merely to contrast his reference to Zachary Grey's 'Hudibras' in the 'Journal of a Voyage to Lisbon' with Warburton's extraordinary abuse of a work to which he himself had contributed, but subsequently described, after his fashion, as—in regard to its notes—'an execrable heap of nonsense.' Of this judgement Nichols not unreasonably observes that if the notes at times treat of insignificant books, the books in question require to be referred to, since they are mentioned by the author annotated—a defence, by the way, which might be advanced in many similar cases where notes are too hastily condemned as needless. Johnson's notice of Cave in the 'Gentleman's Magazine' supplies a two-page comment. This, however, is all we have of Johnson, whom Nichols admired enthusiastically, and whose 'Lives of the Poets' he printed. But if Leviathan be absent, of the lesser fry there is no lack. You shall find something of Fielding's 'Parson Adams,' William Young, concerning

whom—to use a happy expression employed by
the great Dictionary-maker—it may be said that
he had abilities which he possessed rather than
exerted; of Robert Lloyd, who comes in the
same category, and whose lamentable career has
already been summarized in an earlier ingather-
ing of these essays;[1] of the Formosan fraud,
George Psalmanazar; of the curious antiquary
and book-collector, John Bagford, whose letters
with their bad spelling and good matter are still
to be seen at the British Museum; of impostors
such as Bower and Lauder; of divines as diverse
as Dodd and Delany; of pressmen like Bowyer's
connection, Ichabod Dawks, and Dyer of the
news-letters—the 'Dawksque Dyerque' of that
elegant Latinist, Mr. Edmund or 'Rag' Smith
of Christ Church, Oxford; of Ducarel and Peake
and Lort, antiquaries; of Frances Brooke, who
wrote 'Lady Julia Mandeville'; of Shenstone
and Mason, and Melmoth and Spence, and
Churchill and Armstrong, and Jago and Keate,
and some hundreds of others whom to recapitulate would
eclipse
That tedious Tale of HOMER's Ships,
and achieve a Catalogue without the compensat-

---

[1] 'At Prior Park,' 1912, pp. 210-42.

ing advantages of an Index. To-day Bowyer's
'Memoirs' is a book of reference rather than a
book to be read, though read in its own time it
undoubtedly was. Walpole's testimony has already
been heard; and Johnson, writing late in life to
its author that he had been enjoying it at
Ashbourne, describes it as 'full of contemporary
history,' while in an earlier letter, despatched
from 'Brighthelmston' in the year of its publication, he tells him how much he has been informed and gratified. And then he goes on to
say he wishes Nichols would complete the
labours of that eccentric antiquary, Dr. Richard
Rawlinson,[1] who, up to his death, had collected
considerable material in continuation of the
'Athenæ Oxonienses' of Anthony à Wood.

It was part of Nichols' nature to develop
and expand a successful idea ; and the relations
which in 1778 he had formed with the popular
'Gentleman's Magazine' founded by Cave,

---

[1] Dr. R.—according to Nichols—was the perfervid non-
juring Bishop who, having been induced to believe that a
head blown off a spike on Temple Bar had belonged to the
ill-fated Jacobite, Counsellor Christopher Layer, directed
himself to be buried with that misleading memento in his
right hand. But this direction, says the D.N.B., was not
carried out.

greatly enlarged his opportunities for obtaining and securing the particular waif and stray of literary history in which his soul delighted. By 1812-3 his accumulated information had grown to six volumes, which he issued under the general title of 'Literary Anecdotes of the Eighteenth Century.' Bowyer's 'Memoirs' was still the professed kernel of the series, which the title-page further defined as 'comprizing . . . an incidental view of the progress and advancement of literature in this Kingdom during the last century; and biographical anecdotes of a considerable number of eminent writers and ingenious artists.' Three supplementary volumes contained indexes and additions. Yet even this collection did not exhaust its compiler's energy, or material. Between 1817 and 1831 appeared six more volumes of 'Illustrations of the Literary History of the Eighteenth Century.' Two of these were posthumous; and two more were added in 1848 and 1858 by his son, John Bowyer Nichols. The 'Illustrations' include many of Nichols's own letters; but they are scarcely as interesting as the 'Anecdotes.' The format of both, however, makes them more easy to consult than the 'Memoirs of Bowyer,' while their arrangement more nearly coincides with the convenient progression of a work of reference. And whatever their defects may be, they abound in those 'biographical incidents' or 'minute passages of private life' which Johnson defined as 'anecdotes,' and which, in this sense, he told Boswell he loved. Whether, could he have inspected his famous biography, he would have entirely approved his listener's remorseless reading of this admission, as applied to his own presentment, may be doubted; but there must still be many who, with him, relish anecdote in its restrained and regulated form.

The development of the 'Memoirs of Bowyer' has led us far beyond the date of the first appearance of that book in 1782; and the intermediate record of Nichols's activity, both as a printer and antiquary, is closely packed. With the works which he merely printed, we can have little here to do. Neither need we linger on such topographical efforts as the histories of Hinckley and Canonbury, nor on the eight folio volumes which, between 1795 and 1815, he devoted to the county of Leicester, and regarded as his 'most durable monument.' It is rather with his labours as a registrar or interpreter of the literary history of his time that we must deal. Foremost of these come the eight volumes of 'Select Miscellaneous Poems,' with which, in 1780-1782, he supplemented the collections of Dodsley and Pearch, and Johnson's 'Poets,' and which, we are told,[1] contain not a single piece that had previously been printed by their predecessors. In this work he was assisted by Lowth, Percy, and Pope's editor, Thomas Warton. Another important production was the 'Epistolary Correspondence' of Francis Atterbury, 1783-7, which—despite its unscientific arrangement, and the fact that the original letters, now in the Chapter Library at Westminster, have since been reprinted—remains, in its latest form of 1799, an invaluable store of trustworthy information, deserving, in the words of the Bishop's latest and best biographer, Canon Beeching, the 'most ample acknowledgement of obligation.' Nichols also added several hundred lives to the second edition of the 'Biographical Dictionary,' undertaken with Dr. Ralph Heathcote; aided in and prefaced the six-volume 'Tatler' that Calder built out of Percy's material; edited Steele's 'Letters,' and some of his minor efforts—the 'Theatre,' 'Fish-Pool,' 'Town-Talk' and so forth; and was, finally, responsible for a volume containing the works of Leonard Welsted, intended to relieve that luckless verseman and translator of Longinus from Pope's malicious

[1] 'Gentleman's Magazine,' February 1780, pp. 86-89.

'Flow, *Welsted,* flow, like thine inspirer Beer,'
an apparently unwarranted imputation, though
Welsted had unhappily begun the quarrel. But
the enterprise with which, from 1778 onward,
Nichols was most persistently and profitably occupied—an enterprise that, in fact, helped him as
much as he helped it—was the famous omnium
gatherum known as the 'Gentleman's Magazine.'

In 1778 the 'Gentleman's Magazine,' once
fondly described by Johnson as 'a periodical
pamphlet, of which the scheme is known wherever
the English language is spoken,' was more than
forty-seven years old. Since Edward Cave, in
January 1731, had first set up his presses in the
quaint turreted building at Clerkenwell, formerly
the entrance to the Priory of St. John of Jerusalem, the 'Gentleman's Magazine' had gradually
grown to be an established institution, penetrating to the remotest corners of the three king-
doms, flourishing in the face of opposition, improving notwithstanding its prosperity, and
victoriously holding its own against a host of
envious imitators and competitors. 'London'
and 'Universal,' 'Scot's' and 'European'—none
of these or their congeners had any vogue at all
corresponding to that of the blue-covered periodical
which came out regularly at the end of each

month, with a representation of the old Gate-house on its first page. The rude type-metal [?] cut still shows the side-door opening into Cave's offices, and the window of the great room over the archway where (as report affirms) Garrick made his début in Fielding's 'Mock Doctor.' In its earliest form the 'Gentleman's Magazine' bore the sub-title of 'Monthly Intelligencer;' and the putative 'author' was announced as 'Sylvanus Urban, Gent.,' a compound 'nom de guerre' of itself happy enough to absolve its begetter from any imputation of sluggish invention. The initial purpose was simply to give 'Monthly a View of all the Pieces of Wit, Humour, or Intelligence daily offer'd to the Publick' in the swarming news-sheets of which, even at this date, there were in London alone no fewer than two hundred; to add to these things 'Select Pieces of POETRY,'[1] '*Transactions* and

---

[1] The specimens chosen for the first number led off with the 'New-Year's Day Ode' of the recently-appointed laureate, 'C. Cibber, Esq;'. This is followed by an Ode to the same dignitary by Queen Caroline's thresher-poet, 'Stephen Duck, Esq;' according to whom—

'*Phœbus* with joy looks *Britain* round to see
The happy state of his lov'd poetry'—

as evidenced by the glorious elevation of that ' great prince

Events, Foreign and Domestick,' Births, Deaths
and Marriages, etc., ' Prices of *Goods* and *Stock,*'
' Bill of *Mortality,*' ' A Register of Books,' and
' Observations in *Gardening.*' Subject to the
inevitable modifications arising out of expansion
and experience; and the greater originality born
of confidence, this continued to be the staple
matter of the Magazine, since the ' Preface '
to the Index for the first fifty-six volumes,
while dwelling on the growth of the antiquarian
element in the text, lays particular stress on
the permanent value of the Historical Chronicle,
and the records of Books and Pamphlets, especially—as regards the latter—for the period an-
tecedent to the appearance [in 1749] of the
' Monthly Review' of Ralph Griffiths. Many
of the numbers reached five or six editions; and

of comedy and song,' Eusden's successor. Other tributes
are more impartial, if not so flattering. Some of the remaining ' metrifications ' consist of epitaphs on the actress,
Anne Oldfield (a famous impersonator of Cibber's ' Lady
Betty Modish '), who, ' Alive with Peers, with Monarchs
in her Grave,' as Bramston sings, had, not long before,
been magnificently interred in Westminster Abbey—a
strange contrast to her gifted French contemporary,
Adrienne Lecouvreur, who, early in the same year, 1730,
had only found unchristian burial in the Grenouillère, an
obscure corner on the south bank of the Seine.

according to Johnson, the sale in Cave's day was
ten thousand copies. This must have been a very
moderate or a very early estimate, as a far larger
circulation appears to have been attained by some
of Cave's 'invaders.'[1] Nor can they all have
perished prematurely. The 'London Magazine,'
for instance, survived until 1785, and the 'Universal Magazine' until 1803.

With one exception, no collaborator of distinction was at the outset associated with Cave
in his long-planned, but hazardous venture.
Among the early contributors mentioned by Sir
John Hawkins, the most notorious is Samuel
Boyse, author of 'The Deity,' a poem Fielding
praised in the 'Champion' and quoted in 'Tom
Jones.' Boyse is the typical 'distressed poet' of
the period, 'impransus' and improvident—sub-

---

[1] Hill's 'Boswell,' 1887, iii, 322. Johnson perhaps
meant that ten thousand copies made an edition, although
his statement receives confirmation in the verses of an
Oxford Correspondent prefixed to vol. vi (1736):

'Happy in this, that while his Rivals fall,
Ten Thousand Monthly for his Labours call.'

It is difficult to arrive at the exact circulation of these old
periodicals. In the last quarter of the century the 'Town
and Country' was said to be selling at the rate of 15,000
copies per month; the 'Lady's,' 16,000.

sisting precariously between the pawnshop and the sponging-house. When he was starving, he refused to eat his beef without ketchup; and he would lay out his last half-guinea on truffles and mushrooms, which, for want of clothes, he ate in bed.[1] Another was the Clerkenwell 'pencutter,' Moses Browne, author of 'Piscatory Eclogues,' later to become the pioneer editor of Walton's 'Angler,' and, later still, Vicar of Olney, where he had John Newton to his curate. A third was John Duick, also a 'pen-cutter,'[2] who, in the intervals of composing prize-poems for his proprietor, played shuttlecock with him for the good of his health. Hawkins mentions several more names, among which may be cited Akenside; Savage, whose 'Volunteer Laureats' Cave printed; Lockman, afterwards the 'Herring Poet' of Hogarth's 'Beer Street'; and 'Robert Luck, A.M.,' Gay's Barnstaple schoolmaster; but the illustrious exception above referred to is Johnson, of whom we first hear in connection with the

---

[1] Piozzi, 'Anecdotes,' 1826, p. 92. Mrs. Piozzi had these particulars from Johnson.

[2] Two of this obsolete calling invite a note. But Johnson, who knew Browne, gives it no place in his Dictionary. There is only one illustration of the word in the O.E.D., and it is but perfunctorily defined elsewhere.

fifty-pound prize offered by 'Mr. Urban' in
July 1734, for a poem on the comprehensive
theme of 'Life, Death, Judgment, Heaven, and
Hell.' In the November following Johnson wrote
to Cave from Birmingham, under the pseudonym
of 'S. Smith,'[1] offering 'sometimes to fill a column'
with verse or criticism. That Cave replied is
known; but not what he said—though it is quite
possible that Johnson's proposal to do away with
'low jests, aukward buffoonery, or the dull
scurrilities of either party' (some of which things
had already been laid at 'Mr. Urban's' door)
may not have been entirely palatable even to 'a
man of slow parts.' Three years later, however,
Johnson contributed to the magazine the fine ode
'Ad Urbanum' beginning:

> URBANE, nullis fesse laboribus,
> URBANE, nullis victe calumniis—

which, besides other happy things, includes, for
its penultimate stanza—

> Non ulla Musis pagina gratior,
> Quam quæ severis ludicra jungere
> Novit, fatigatamque nugis
> Utilibus recreare mentem—

---

[1] This must have been one of Johnson's earliest letters.
It was sold at Christie's in June 1888 for three guineas.
What would be its price now?

surely the best of all mottoes for a popular mis-
cellany! Cave, who was a Rugby boy, must
have appreciated the scholarly compliment, for
the verses appeared in the 'Gentleman's' for
March 1738; and henceforth, says Boswell, that
magazine was, during many years Johnson's
'principal source for employment and support.'
His work was of all sorts, and frequently edi-
torial; but for a considerable time his best ascertained duties were the reporting, under the
heading of 'The Senate of Lilliput,' of the
debates in Parliament. Johnson was at first employed simply to revise the rough records brought
home from memory by one of Ralph's 'Authors
by Profession,' a certain Guthrie, with whom
this matter had previously rested; but as Johnson
'more and more enriched' the speeches in re-
casting them, the task at last fell wholly into his
hands, and for some three years he was their
'sole composer.' After him, they were continued
by Hawkesworth and others; and, in this form,
finally faded out altogether in 1746. In the
Preface of 1747 they are described as belonging
to a time when 'a determined spirit of opposition
in the national assemblies communicated itself to
almost every individual, multiplied and invigor-
ated periodical papers, and rendered politics the

chief, if not the only, object of curiosity'—to which Dr. Birkbeck Hill adds that 'they are a monument to the greatness of Walpole, and to the genius of Johnson.' During the same period Johnson wrote several admirable short biographies, *e.g.* of Father Sarpi (whose history of the Council of Trent he had begun to translate), of Boerhaave, Drake, Sydenham, Roscommon, and Savage, besides numerous miscellaneous papers, some acknowledged, others assigned to him on internal evidence. Among the latter are included Prefaces to separate volumes, more than one of which deal trenchantly with the manners and methods of 'Mr. Urban's' unscrupulous rivals.[1]

In January 1754 Cave died; and Johnson, then hard at work on the 'Dictionary,' wrote an obituary notice in the February number of the magazine, to which was prefixed the well-known etching by Worlidge after Kyte's portrait. By this time the 'Gentleman's' had entered on its twenty-fourth volume; and was regarded as 'one of the most successful and lucrative pamphlets which literary history has upon record.' The last assertion is indirectly confirmed by the inscription on the monument erected to him in

[1] See especially volumes for 1738 and 1739.

Rugby churchyard, which states that it brought him 'an ample Fortune.' At Cave's death the magazine passed into the hands of David Henry, a young printer who had married his sister; and Henry, in conjunction with Cave's nephew, Richard Cave, carried on the business. Johnson continued to assist; and detailed reviews began to take the place of the old bare list of books. Fresh contributors were also found in Christopher Smart, Dr. James of the Fever Powders, Hill of the 'Inspector,' and John Newbery, 'the philanthropic bookseller of St. Paul's Churchyard' (as Goldsmith calls him). When, in 1766, Richard Cave died, Francis Newbery's name appeared in the title-page; and twelve years later, after Henry had transferred his printing work to an agent, John Nichols became definitely associated in the management. From this date, indeed, until a short time before his death in 1826 Nichols virtually acted as editor, taking the keenest interest in the fortunes and development of the concern, and contributing regularly on all topics, either over his initials or a pseudonym. Cave, Johnson said, 'never looked out of his window, but with a view to the 'Gentleman's Magazine'; and in this kind of vigilance Nichols was his worthy successor, besides being far more of an 'editor'—

as that term is now understood. Of course he
depended largely upon an ever-increasing staff of
correspondents,[1] and it is quite conceivable that
his material was not invariably of permanent
value;[2] but there is no doubt that to his unwearied assiduity in collecting and selecting it is
due that the 'Gentleman's Magazine' acquired
the reputation it enjoyed in the final quarter of
the eighteenth century of being the most trustworthy existing repertory of current Literature,
Science, Topography, Antiquities, and Biography,
—the last three especially. Its value in these
respects was considerably increased by the 'General
Index' to the first fifty-six volumes compiled in
1789 by the Rev. Samuel Ayscough, Assistant
Librarian of the British Museum. To this was
prefixed a preface prepared by Johnson for an
earlier occasion. More than thirty years later a
further Index, carrying the record to 1818, was

[1] Cowper's delightful description of his three hares,
Puss, Tiney and Bess, appeared in the 'Gentleman's' for
June 1784, and the epitaph on Tiney followed in Dec-
ember.

[2] But Southey, writing from Keswick in 1804, and
complaining of the 'exquisite inanity' of the magazine,
and the 'glorious and intense stupidity of its correspondence,' is certainly expecting too much or going too far
(' Life and Correspondence,' 1849-50, ii, 281).

Q

published; when Nichols, being then seventy-six, contributed a leisurely introduction describing the rise and progress of the periodical, and embodying many discursive details bearing on its history. In a longer paper some of these might find a place. We can only refer to two. One is the curious admission contained in a correspondence between Richardson and Cave regarding Johnson's 'Rambler' (which Cave printed) that neither of those lettered worthies, on their own showing, had ever read more than a few numbers of the 'Spectator'; the other involves the disclosure of Nichols himself as a versifier. In the volume for 1784—anticipating Mr. Toots, and taking on him a becoming 'superbia quaesita meritis'—he addressed the following sonnet to himself:

URBAN, thy skill matur'd by mellowing Time,
　Thy pleasing toil, thy well-conducted page,
Through Britain's Realms, and many a Foreign
　　　Clime,
　Have charm'd the last, and charm the present age.
Unnumber'd Rivals, urg'd by thy renown,
　To match thy useful labours oft have tried;
In vain they tried; unnotic'd and unknown,
　In cold Oblivion's shade they sunk, and died.
Chear'd by the fostering beams of public praise,
　Continue still 'to profit and delight';

Whilst Learning all her ample store displays,
  Her 'varying' charms at thy command 'unite.'
Hence future Hawkesworths, Wartons, Grays may sing,
Where virtuous JOHNSON plum'd his eagle wing.

That this unlocking of its writer's heart is
more than respectable, can scarcely be claimed.
But it is noteworthy on other grounds. Besides
preserving the mottoes of the magazine—' Prod-
esse et delectare' and ' E pluribus unum '—it is
interesting from the fact that Nichols submitted
it to Johnson at his last interview with him. His
old friend, among other farewell injunctions,
adjured him, as he had adjured Reynolds, not to
work on Sunday. ' Remember to observe the
Sabbath,' he said; ' let it not be a day of business, nor wholly a day of dissipation '; and he
added that his words should have their due weight,
as they were ' those of a dying man.' [1]

After the ' Gentleman's Magazine,' of which
the later story belongs to our own days,[2] there is
not much more to say of Nichols as a ' littérateur.'
' Nullis fessus laboribus '—like his predecessor—
he continued to exert his praiseworthy activities,

[1] General Index to the ' Gentleman's Magazine,' 1821,
iii, lxiii, n. In the magazine the sonnet is followed by a
reprint of Johnson's ode 'Ad Urbanum.'

[2] It only came to an end in the present century.

reaping in due time the recompense of the diligent, and becoming successively Common Coun-
cillor, Deputy of his Ward, Master of the
Stationers' Company, Registrar of the Royal
Literary Fund, Governor of this or that charity
—and so forth.   Not the least of his distinctions,
perhaps, was that he belonged to Johnson's last
club at the Essex Head.   With Dogberry, he had
his losses; and, in 1808, he suffered heavily by a
fire, which destroyed the bulk of his stock.   But
he outlived this calamity more than eighteen
years.   On the 26th of November 1826, he died
suddenly in his house at Highbury Place, leaving
an irreproachable record for integrity and in-
dustry; and the reputation of having successfully
contributed by 'his pleasing toil' and 'well-conducted page' to the instruction and gratification
of many thousands of his contemporaries.

AARON HILL

WHAT can possibly have been the phreno-
logical 'bumps' of the man who christened
his helpless offspring Minerva, Urania, Astraea,
and Julius Caesar! It is a nice speculation; and
one which might have interested Charles Lamb.
But the biographical field offers to the sportsman
bigger game than AARON HILL; and the enquiry
has been neglected. From time to time, indeed,
he has been heard of; but hardly with sympathy.
To Sir Leslie Stephen—not often impatient—he
is a 'bore of the first water'; and another distinguished critic, the late D. C. Tovey, defines him
(surely somewhat euphuistically) as 'a practical
joke concocted between the Muses and Momus,
to bring the judgments of mortals into contempt,'[1]
though he admits that Hill was 'once a power
in the world of letters,' while even the earlier
critic concedes to him both courtesy and amiability. And now, at last, he has found a fitting
chronicler. From Miss Dorothy Brewster's[2]

[1] Thomson's 'Works,' 1897, i, xxiii.
[2] 'Aaron Hill, Poet, Dramatist, Projector.' By Dorothy Brewster, Ph.D. New York, Columbia University

careful and laborious pages, he emerges as a far more interesting personality than would have been imagined. If he was not conspicuously eminent as the poet, dramatist and projector of her sub-title—if he was scarcely the 'supreme genius' of his friend Thomson's grateful 'deference and veneration,' he was, at least, a kindly and im-pulsive enthusiast; more ambitious, it may be, than able; more assimilative than inventive; but of endless ingenuity and indefatigable energy. He is an exemplification of Taine's dictum that, in literature as in war, 'the common soldiers occa-sionally exhibit, more clearly than the generals, the capabilities and tendencies of their time and country.' From this point of view alone, Aaron Hill deserves the fuller consideration he has recently received.

He was born on the 10th of February 1685, at a house on the site of Beaufort Buildings in the Strand. His father, George Hill of Malmesbury Abbey, Wiltshire, was an attorney, originally of a good estate, which he gradually dissipated, leav-ing, at his death, the education of his children to

Press, 1913. This book has been approved by the De-partment of English and Comparative Literature in Columbia University 'as a contribution to knowledge worthy of publication.'

his widow and her mother. Aaron's first school-
ing was at Barnstaple, under Mr. Rayner, where
he had to his school-fellow, John Gay, the
fabulist. From Barnstaple he passed to Westminster, then under Busby's successor, Dr. Knipe.
One of his contemporaries, Barton Booth, became
the actor and impersonator of Addison's 'Cato';
another was the future Lord Carteret. The only
tradition surviving from these days is that Hill
increased his slender pocket money by doing the
tasks of his classmates, an occupation which his
biographer suggests was probably more profitable
commercially than some of his later enterprises.
At fourteen he left Westminster; and discovering that he possessed an influential relative in the
person of Lord Paget (the fifth baron), King
William's Ambassador to Turkey, persuaded his
grandmother to let him visit his lordship. In
March 1700 he accordingly set out, by way of
Portugal and Italy, for Constantinople—a remarkable expedition for a lad of fifteen, however pre-
cocious. He was apparently well-grown and good-
looking, points which, no doubt, told in his favour,
for, contrary to all precedent, Lord Paget received
him with much cordiality, and equipped him with
a tutor or Governor, with whom he sent him to
travel in the East. The journal of his voyage to

the Turkish capital is lost; but many particulars
of what constitutes his Oriental Grand Tour are
scattered through the description of the 'Ottoman
Empire' which he issued eight years later. From
these it appears that he explored Greece and the
Islands of the Ægean; went by caravan into the
Holy Land; visited Mecca and Jerusalem, and
was all but assassinated by a Mohammedan fanatic.
Other excursions were made to Sestos and Abydos;
to the reputed site of Troy and Hector's tomb.
At Samos he watched the sponge-divers, and
although 'more than most men averse to diving,'
endeavoured to emulate them; at Patmos he for-
gathered with an Italian hermit, much less gloomy
than his cell; and narrowly escaped being en-
tombed in the catacombs near Memphis, which
were then made use of by the predatory Arabs as
death-traps for the unsuspecting traveller. After
these experiences—probably more or less romanced
in the telling—he returned home in Lord Paget's
suite, reaching England, after a circuitous and leisurely journey through the Continent, on the 12th
of April 1703, the passage from Holland having
been 'enlivened by a sea-fight with the French.'

By this time he was eighteen, and of the next
few years no very definite record exists. But it is
clear that his status in the Paget household was

disturbed by 'the malice of a certain female,' not
more explicitly described; and that his next occupation was that of tutor to a young gentleman
of the Wentworth family, with whom he travelled
abroad for three or four years, returning about
1706-7, having greatly improved his pupil, and,
on his own part, having gained impressions considerably more mature than those he had previously collected. His next connection was with
that eccentric and ubiquitous personage, Charles,
Earl of Peterborough and Monmouth (Swift's
'Mordanto'), to some 'the ramblingest lying
rogue on earth'; to others, a Paladin of romance.
After the capture of Barcelona, Peterborough was
recalled by Queen Anne; and his conduct in
Spain became the subject of an inconclusive
Parliamentary enquiry. His exploits and his
Quixotic personality were just of the kind to
attract Hill, who, in 1707, addressed to him,
under the title of 'Camillus,' a laudatory poem
in heroics, his first effort in this way, but possessing little value save its enthusiasm. Here and
there one lights upon a compact couplet, for
example, that describing Spain as

> Made poor, by *plenty*, dull *content* she knew;
> Her strength *declining*, as her riches *grew*.

which might—without its intrusive italics—have

come from Goldsmith's 'Traveller'; while the
not-inappropriate lines on Peterborough himself:

> He needs no *council,* and he seeks no *praise:*
> When *other* generals *tedious* projects *form,*
> He *thinks,* and *acts,* and *wins* applause, by *storm,*

must have pleased his erratic hero. At all events,
Peterborough made the young man his secretary,
a post which Hill retained until 1710. The
interval, when not absorbed by his duties, was
devoted to letters. He became a frequenter of
the coffee houses; and companioned with Tate
(the Laureate), and his old schoolfellow Gay, who,
at one time, is supposed to have been *his* secretary.
He wrote occasional and amatory verses; celebrated, in 'The Invasion,' the Pretender's un-
successful attempt on Scotland in 1708; helped
Tate to translate parts of Ovid's 'Metamorphoses,'
and contributed to that curious forerunner of
Steele's 'Tatler,' the 'British Apollo,' a species
of Augustan 'Enquire Within,' which had not
only considerable success, but many successors.
His most ambitious effort, however, was his 'Full
and Just Account of the Present State of the
Ottoman Empire,' 1709, already referred to, a
stately folio based on his Oriental travels, having
seven plates (each frugally dedicated to a noble
patron), and preceded by a goodly subscription

list, including more than four hundred names.
The style is described as pretentious and immature;
the matter often reminiscent of Rycaut and others,
though the passages which bear on his personal
experiences have freshness and novelty. Hill himself eventually grew ashamed of this performance,
professing to regard it—rather late in the day—
as a boyish effort for which it was unjust to render
him accountable; but it reached a second edition
in 1710. This was the year of the author's
marriage to Miss Morris, an Essex lady of fortune,
an event which also marks the interruption, though
not the termination, of his connection with Lord
Peterborough, who wished to carry his secretary
with him to the West Indies. This proposition
was, however, so strongly opposed by Mrs. Hill
that her husband was emboldened to decline it.

His wife's means repaired the lack of any
paternal inheritance; and for some time left him
at liberty to indulge his tastes, literary and otherwise, from the comfortable foot-hold of financial
security. In a projecting age (one remembers
Defoe's 'Essay on Projects'), he was first and
foremost a projector, always, to use an expression
of Mrs. Thrale, 'racking his invention raw'
over some new expedient for benefiting humanity.
But as, unhappily, most of his projects came to

nothing, we may, with some violation of chrono-
logy, imitate his biographer in disposing once for
all, though with greater brevity, of his efforts in
this direction. His first scheme, that, in fact,
with which he is most usually associated, was for
extracting oil from beech-nuts. For this, share-
holders were obtained, money was raised, and
elaborate machinery devised; but the enterprise
collapsed, owing to the unexpected, though
not unprecedented, failure, for a sequence of
years, of the requisite supply of mast. On the
beech-oil fiasco came a society (apparently consisting of himself) for publishing accounts of
new inventions, in which he is identified with
the manufacture of china (from pipe-clay, or
other broken china ground small); with a new
fuel (always a subject of contemporary solicitude!)
to be compacted of coal-dust and Thames mud;
and incidentally with the repairing of that en-
croachment of the Thames near Barking known
as Dagenham Breach, a feat which was successfully performed by Captain John Perry.[1] Vine-

---

[1] With the periodical inspections of the embankment
works at Dagenham Breach originated the Ministerial
Whitebait dinners, which down to 1870 flourished first
at the Breach House at Dagenham, and afterwards at
Greenwich ('Notes and Queries,' 1 September 1855).

growing in England was another of his dreams.
Then he is Treasurer for the Golden Islands in
Carolina where gentlemen from England and
America were invited to settle under attractive
inducements and special immunities—a scheme
which, like the rest, failed, but was effected later
to some extent by Oglethorpe's colonization of
Georgia. Next he is agent for the York Buildings Company; and occupied in the importation
of timber and other commodities from Scotland,
with collateral activities in the manufacture of
potash. But here again the results failed to realize
the expectations formed. By this time Hill's
losses and disappointments had considerably
cooled his ardour for company-promoting and
projects generally; and he came at last to the
conclusion that he would 'have done with all
designs he could not execute himself.' He was
still 'chock-full of science' (as Captain Cuttle
would say); but his enthusiasm was scarcely as
inflammable as of yore. In quitting this aspect
of his career, it is but fair to add that he was far
removed from the ordinary speculator, and genuinely desirous of benefiting his fellow men. He
took infinite pains to qualify himself for the researches he engaged upon; and if his inventions
exhausted his energy, and drained his purse, he

seems to have regretted, not so much his own
waste of time and money, as the loss to the public of those incalculable advantages he had endeavoured to secure for them.

In carrying on the story of Hill's projects, it
has been necessary to anticipate. But though his
'projects' illustrate his character, they are by no
means the most attractive part of it; and to 'have
done' with them (as he did), leaves one free to
take up his connection with theatrical affairs and
with his literary contemporaries, especially Pope
and Richardson. In regard to the stage, his first
beginnings are obscure. But as his earliest tragedy
of 'Elfrid; or, the Fair Inconstant,' is said to
have been written at the desire of Barton Booth,
the actor, who, as already related, had been his
schoolmate at Westminster, it is perhaps only
reasonable to associate Booth with his first dramatic beginnings. At all events, from the
troubled rivalries of Drury Lane and the Haymarket, then the only London theatres, he issues
suddenly in November 1709, as Manager and
Director of Drury Lane, at that date under the
jurisdiction of one of the patentees, William Collier, M.P. How Hill obtained this important
position, and why, are not stated; but he held it
from the above date to June 1710. During this

period, as might be predicted, he produced three
pieces of his own, the aforesaid tragedy of
'Elfrid' (to which, in its revised form, we shall
again refer); a comedy, 'Trick upon Trick; or,
'Squire Brainless'; and a farce, 'The Walking
Statue,' the most successful of the three, although
Genest gives it the dubious commendation of
being 'more amusing to watch than it is to read'
—praise which suggests the cinematograph rather
than the footlights. As regards ''Squire Brainless,' notwithstanding Hill's assertion that comedy
is 'the easiest way of pleasing,' it was acted but
three times, and never printed, facts which seem
to indicate that, facility apart, its author's bent
was rather to the buskin than the sock. Fortunately he did not confine his managerial efforts to
his own performances; but successfully revived
several old plays, and produced some new ones.
Of these latter was Charles Shadwell's 'Fair
Quaker of Deal; or, The Humours of the Navy,'
which, with its Flips and Mixens, follows Con-
greve and anticipates Smollett in its graphic presentment of the seaman of the period. Even
during the Sacheverell trial of 1710, Shadwell's
comedy drew crowds to Drury Lane. Then
came the inevitable dissensions in the company,
culminating in a riot, the result being that Hill

transferred his energies to the Haymarket and to Opera, an arrangement facilitated by the fortune which at this time he acquired by his marriage.

Opera, in England at this date (1710), was in a languishing way. But Hill's first experiences were of happy augury. After many solicitations, Handel was paying his first visit to this country, and Hill at once approached him. A subject was selected from Tasso's 'Gerusalemme Liberata'; an Italian libretto was prepared by Giacomo Rossi, which Hill translated; and for this Handel composed the opera of 'Rinaldo,' which, with much splendour of 'Scenes and Machines,' was produced at the Haymarket, and received with great enthusiasm. It ran from February to June. The 'British Apollo' floridly commended the 'vast, extended mind' of the youthful manager, and the ingenuity of those living birds, spitting dragons, and real waterfalls in the decorations, concerning which Mr. Joseph Addison, in the new paper the 'Spectator,' perhaps remembering ruefully the failure of a certain 'Rosamond' of his own, was pleased to be ironic. He objected, also, to 'Seignior [1] *Hendel's*' being described as the '*Orpheus* of our Age,' in which he proved himself an incompetent prophet. 'Rinaldo,'

---

[1] He corrected this in the next number to 'Minheer.'

however, was not a maintained success. Handel went back to Hanover; Hill was displaced and for the next few years was absorbed by his beech-oil project. Not till February 1716 did he return to the stage with 'The Fatal Vision; or, the Fall of Siam,' which was produced at Lincoln's Inn Fields, and played seven times. Both plot and fable are fictitious. But despite its dedication to the two critics, Dennis and Gildon, and despite the mingling of French regularity with 'fulness of design,' its author seems to have had no further resource than to go back to his inventions. When he re-visited the boards, five years later, it was to oblige a needy Scotch friend, Joseph Mitchell, Walpole's poet, in whose name his work appeared. The 'Fatal Extravagance' (Hill seems fond of the epithet) was based on the 'Yorkshire Tragedy,' the best of the six spurious plays attributed to Shakespeare. It was acted—according to Mallet—'with a great deal of applause'; and must have lightened the liabilities of its necessitous foster-father.

The success of the 'Fatal Extravagance' seems to have swept Hill once more into matters theatric. But it is impossible to enter the maze of his managerial experiences. His next personal essay in the direction of 'fulness of design' and

R

the maintenance of the unities, was an ill-judged
and pretentious re-casting of Shakespeare's
'Henry V.'[1] That the 'Biographia Dramatica'
should call this 'a very good play,' is incompre-
hensible; but it is undoubtedly an excellent example of eighteenth-century adaptation. The
unities are conciliated by laying the scene wholly
in France; Fluellen, Pistol, Gower and so forth,
disappear; and the gross 'rusticity' of Henry's
courtship of Katharine of France is combed out
and curled to suit the Georgian standard of elegance. Worse than all, a new character is added
in the person of an entirely superfluous Harriet,
niece of Lord Scroop. In these things Hill did
no more than his contemporaries—as Otway
before and Cumberland after him; and in obedi-
ence to Gallic models. He and his school had
not the faintest idea that they were not improving
Voltaire's 'amiable barbarian'; and he was seriously wounded when a certain 'Menander' in
'Pasquin' (for there were some good Shake-

[1] 'One can foretell with some accuracy,' writes Miss
Brewster, 'what eighteenth century adapters will cut out
of a Shakespearean play, but only a genius akin to their
own can conceive what they will put in.' As an instance
of inane excision, she notes: 'Tarry, sweet soul, for
mine; then fly abreast,' from Exeter's account of the
deaths of York and Suffolk (act iv, sc. 6).

speareans even in 1723) raised the remonstrance
of common sense. The majority of Hill's audience, however, considered that he was 'Shakespeare by transmigration.' Yet not even Booth's
costume and Anne Oldfield's charms could prolong the vogue of ' Henry V ' beyond six nights.

It was perhaps only in the nature of things that
Hill chose to attribute this failure of ' Henry V '
to causes other than its inherent defects. That it
did not succeed, he held, was owing to the disastrous popularity of dumb show—of the sense-
less Pantomime and Harlequinade which John
Rich had made the reigning fashion.[1] At all
events, he was silenced for the next few years.
Then, in 1731, the favour shown to Mallet's
' Eurydice ' and Thomson's ' Sophonisba ' led him
to remodel his tragedy of ' Elfrid ' under the new
name of ' Athelwold.' But the further complica-
tion of the plot and the additional incidents were
as powerless as the advocacy of Pope and Peterborough. It ran but three nights. Hill consequently determined to ' leave the loathéd Stage '
in the capacity of playwright; and to devote
himself to the more agreeable task of criticizing
its shortcomings. To this end he established the

[1] Hogarth satirized Rich's ' *dumb* Faustus ' in ' Masquerades and Operas,' 1724.

periodical known as 'The Prompter,' 1734-6.
It treated of many subjects, social and literary;
but its main haunt and region was the footlights.
It has been compactly praised as being the 'best
contemporary criticism of an interesting situation,' to wit, the condition of the Georgian
theatre before the advent of Garrick. Many of
Hill's theories are now mossed into truisms; but
he was then far better informed than his contemporaries. Plays and players are alike dissected—
the latter so pointedly as to provoke occasional
reprisals. Cibber, in tragedy, was likened to 'an
unjointed caterpillar,' at which that impenitent
veteran only laughed; but the 'deliberate and
solemn' Quin did not relish being nicknamed
'Mr. All-weight,' and came to undignified blows
with his censor. Personalities, however, were
the exception; and Hill's more general arraign-
ment of the incompetence and intrigues of the
managers; of the immoral character of the
plays; of those 'wild triumphs of Folly,' Panto-
mimes and Entertainments; of the stilted mouth-
ing of the male actors and the lachrymose whine
of the women; of the disorderly behaviour of the
audience and the tyranny of the footmen's gallery
—all these things are of the most pertinent and
instructive kind. 'Similar opinions are scattered

through the plays, periodicals, letters, and pamphlets of the day, but the "Prompter's" value is that it focuses them all.'[1] It deserves to be better known.

Hill's only other dramatic efforts that matter are his translations from Voltaire. These were three in number, 'Zara,' 1736; 'Alzira,' 1736; and 'Merope,' 1749. 'Zara' was produced at Drury Lane in January 1736, and ran fourteen nights. This, for Hill, amounted to a triumph. His version, it is admitted, was skilful, and its success was secured by the acting of the leading lady, the beautiful Susanna Maria Cibber, who had been Hill's pupil.[2] In the 'Dedication' to the second French edition Voltaire politely referred to his English translator as 'M. Hill, homme de lettres, qui paraît connaître le théâtre mieux qu'aucun auteur anglais.' Voltaire's 'Zaire,' it is to be observed, is not without obligations to Shakespeare. But what concerns us here is that Hill's adaptation of it is his best effort. A few months later he produced another version of

---

[1] 'Aaron Hill,' p. 125.

[2] 'Zaire' is one of the best of Voltaire's tragedies; and its author also professed himself to be highly indebted to the 'large black eyes' and Oriental elegance of Mlle. Jeanne Gaussin, who personated the heroine.

Voltaire, ' Alzira.' It ran nine nights. After this
a difference arose between Voltaire and his
English admirer; Voltaire had written a ' Mort
de César ' (based on Shakespeare's ' ouvrage
monstrueux '), and to counteract it Hill wrote
the ' Roman Revenge,' which was not acted
during his lifetime. His last translation or variation from Voltaire was ' Merope,' which Garrick
produced at Drury Lane in 1749, taking himself the part of Dorilas.[1] Hill's preface to ' Merope ' shows his altered attitude to Voltaire, who
had prefixed to the French original a depreciation of English tragedy. ' Il semble (he said) que
la même cause qui prive les Anglais du génie de
la peinture, et de la musique, leur ôte aussi celui
de la tragédie.' Hill retorted: ' He [Voltaire]
must pardon me, if I am sensible that our un-
polished London stage . . . has entertained a
nobler taste of dignified simplicity than to de-
prive dramatic poetry of all that animates its
passions,[2] in pursuit of a cold, starved, tame

---

[1] In later years he acted Zara's father, Lusignan.
Dr. Thomas Campbell saw him in this part in March
1775 (' Diary ' in Napier's ' Johnsoniana,' 1884, p. 243).

[2] Voltaire disapproved of love-episodes in the more
elevated tragedy. The motto to the first edition of
' Mérope ' was: ' Hoc legite, austeri; crimen amoris abest';

abstinence; which, from an affectation to shun figure, sinks to flatness; an elaborate escape from energy into a grovelling, wearisome, bald, barren, unalarming, chillness of expression, that emasculates the mind instead of moving it.' Hill is in earnest and sees his points; but Voltaire's unqualified directness is unhappily more damaging than his adversary's clutter of epithets.

'Merope' was Hill's last acted tragedy. It is pleasant to turn from his fruitless projects and dramatic failures to the more congenial story of his many friendships. And here we must retrace our steps to the periodical with which some of these are connected. In March 1724, mainly as a charitable enterprise, he had established the 'Plain Dealer,' a paper on the model of the 'Spectator.' He had a colourless collaborator named Bond; but the better part of the undertaking was his own. The ostensible object was, as usual, 'to advance learning, virtue, and politeness.' In its character-sketches it closely followed its great predecessor, and it dealt with many similar topics, as good breeding, true and false art, decency, patriotism, duelling, and 'phrases a double entente,' into which last it, nevertheless,

and in the 'Mort de César' there were no female characters.

occasionally lapsed. On various subjects it spoke out. It disapproved capital punishment as strenuously as Dickens; with Lady Mary it advocated inoculation; but dealt playfully with 'Woman's Rights.'' Here, however, we may leave Hill's biographer to speak: 'No. 69 is a paper on Woman's Rights. . . . Even Patty Amble herself was probably amused at her own oratory: "How are we represented, when none of our sex are permitted to sit and vote for us? Is this free government? Is this to be subject to no laws but those we have first given consent to? Either let us as a distinct body have a right to govern ourselves; or admit an equal number of us to sit where laws are made for us. And I believe I may venture to undertake . . . that we will be modest enough in that case, to content ourselves with a bare negative upon all bills that concern us." It is interesting to see a joke become in a couple of centuries a great political problem; no bare negative will satisfy the Patty Ambles of to-day.' [1]

One of the most attractive features of the 'Plain Dealer' is Hill's generous and indeed effusive recognition of contemporary talent. For instance, he admired and praised Young's 'Sa-

[1] 'Aaron Hill,' p. 160.

tires '; and it has been suggested by Young's French biographer, Mons. Thomas—on no very strong evidence, it is true—that the future author of the 'Night Thoughts' actually contributed to Hill's paper. Another writer frequently mentioned is Pope's 'Appius,' John Dennis, to whom with Gildon, Hill had dedicated the 'Fatal Vision.' Hill had evidently the greatest admiration for the untunable 'Sir Longinus' as a critic, although he was perfectly alive to his defects. Appealing to Pope in his defence he says: 'Neither of us would choose him for a friend; but none of the frailties of his temper, any more than the heavy formalities of his style, can prevent your acknowledging there is often weight in his arguments, and matter that deserves encouragement to be met with in his writings.'[1] Whether Dennis and Young were Hill's allies or not, it is clear that Hill appreciated the better verse and criticism of his day. He showed his further appreciation of poetry by his recognition of Mallet's 'William and Margaret,' which he reprinted, professedly from a torn leaf of a halfpenny ballad 'Garland' picked up on Primrose Hill; and he espoused the cause of that spoiled child of misfortune, Richard Savage, to whose 'Miscellaneous

---

[1] Hill to Pope, 10 February 1731.

Poems and Translations by Several Hands, 1726, he was the chief contributor. For those who helped him, Savage must have been a trial which it needed all his personal charm to overcome. Among other members of the Hill coterie was Thomson, in the appearance of whose 'Winter' Hill actively interested himself, to be repaid by the then friendless and unknown author with an extravagant gratitude which Johnson regarded as 'servile adulation.' Then there were ladies, Pope's 'Eliza,' Mrs. Haywood (of the 'Secret Histories'); the beautiful 'Clio' or 'Mira' (Miss Martha Fowke); and 'Miranda' (Mrs. Hill)— all equally admiring and admired. Hill gushed; and they gushed responsive. But Hill (or 'Hillarius' as he was affectionately called) was the leader of the band, which, no doubt, periodically performed, greatly to its own gratification, at his pleasant house in Petty France, overlooking St. James's Park—the old St. James's Park of Duck Island and the Canal.[1]

Hill's most prolonged relations, however, were

---

[1] Hill's garden must have been terminated by the park wall (Hill to Pope, 7 November 1733). Pope visited Hill at Westminster, whence Hill sent (or proposed to send) the materials for an obelisk of Jersey shells as an additional adornment of the 'Twittenham' paradise.

with Richardson and Pope. And in the case of Pope, the word 'relations' seems more appropriate than friendship, for friendship it was not —at all events at the outset. In 1718 Hill wrote a poem entitled 'The Northern Star,' on that '*new Cæsar* on the Russian throne,' Peter the Great. By the author's desire, Bernard Lintot, the publisher, submitted it informally to Pope, who praised it faintly, but on political grounds deprecated its publication. Thereupon Hill, mortified exceedingly, printed the piece with an angry 'Preface to Mr. Pope,' of which Pope apparently took no notice. Two years later, Hill sent Pope a poem on 'The Creation,' being a paraphrase of the first chapter of Genesis; and Pope, replying in general terms, took occasion to apologize for his alleged action in the matter of 'The Northern Star.' Hill, completely disarmed, made profuse recantation in a second Preface, in which he said : 'I look up to you with extraordinary comfort, as to a new constellation breaking out upon our world with equal heat and brightness, and cross-spangling, as it were, the whole heaven of wit with your Milky Way of genius.'

After this, things seem to have gone on smoothly until, in March 1728, Hill, to his annoyance, found himself indicated by his initials in the second book and sixth chapter of the 'Memoirs of Martinus Scriblerus,' as belonging to the group of Flying Fishes—'writers who now and then rise upon their fins, and fly out of the profund; but their wings are soon dry, and they drop down to the bottom.' Hill at once retaliated in the 'Daily Journal' by splenetic verses on Pope and Swift. Matters were not mended by the appearance in the 'Dunciad,' a month later, of the following:

> H . . . tried the next, but hardly snatched from sight,
> Instant buoys up, and rises into light;
> He bears no token of the sabler streams,
> And mounts far off among the swans of Thames.

The reference was to the discreditable diving-match of Book II, and, in the next edition (1729), stars replaced the 'H. . .' and the following note was appended to the passage: 'This is an instance of the tenderness of our author. The person here intended writ an angry preface against him, founded on a mistake, which he afterwards honourably acknowledged in another printed preface. Since when he fell under a second mistake, and abused both him and his friend. He is a writer of genius and spirit, though in his youth he was guilty of some pieces bordering upon bombast. Our poet gives him a panegyric instead of a satire, being edified beyond measure by the only instance he ever met with in his life of one who was much a poet confessing himself in an error; and has suppressed his name as thinking him capable of a second repentance.'

The above was proposed as an 'amende'; but Hill could not regard it as entirely 'honorable.' What he disliked—and very naturally disliked— was being included in the diving-match at all. His 'second repentance' took the form of a pseudonymous 'Progress of Wit: a Caveat.' 'For the Use of an Eminent Writer.' It was, in the main, complimentary to Pope, who figured as its 'tuneful Alexis'; but it contained the following couplets representing him as one who:

> Desiring, and deserving, others' praise,
> Poorly accepts a fame he ne'er repays;
> Unborn to cherish, sneakingly approves,
> And wants the soul to spread the worth he loves.

Having thus liberated his mind in rhyme, Hill wrote to Pope, enclosing among other things a poem by his daughter, Urania, aged eleven; and intimating incidentally that he had been pained by the note in the 'Dunciad.' Pope replied in

his usual equivocal way. The note was really an
'oblique panegyric,' though he was not the writer
of it. And then he, on his part, professed to be
hurt by the charge in the 'Caveat' (which he of
course associated with Hill) that he neglected to
cherish or befriend men of merit. Hill rejoined
by a long and manly letter. In this he undoubtedly scored, as, being more straightforward
and sincere than his correspondent, he was bound
to do. Pope's answer was unsatisfactory; but he
accompanied it by a peace-offering in the form of
a copy of the 'Odyssey' for 'Miss Urania.' In a
further letter Hill sent Pope a poem to criticise,
and Pope complied. He evidently feared Hill;
and henceforth substituted the mask of friendship
for open hostility. Hill's copious communications
must have been a terrible infliction; but it was
an infliction to be endured. And endure it Pope
did—with mute intervals—for some eight years,
his last printed letter being dated 1739. It involved him in more than one discreditable side-
issue; and, what was worse, condemned him to
the criticism and re-criticism of 'Athelwold' and
'Cæsar,' into which ordeal Bolingbroke was also
inveigled by their indefatigable author. It is piti-
able to think of Bolingbroke and Pope's giving
their nights and days to the 'Roman Revenge'!

And during most of the time Hill dangled
over Pope's head a never completed 'Essay on
Propriety and Impropriety, in Design, Thought,
and Expression, illustrated by Examples in both
Kinds from the Writings of Mr. Pope'—a performance in which Pope was acute enough to
guess that the improprieties might be far more
trying than the proprieties. The pact, it is clear,
was always hollow. Each distrusted the other;
and there are passages in Hill's letters to Richardson after Pope's death which show unmistakably
that Hill's worship of Pope as a writer had many
reservations, and a substratum of lingering re-
sentment.

The Pope correspondence ceased in 1739,
probably because—as Mr. Courthope conjectures
—Pope was 'tired out with the length of his
penance.' The catastrophe was perhaps precipi-
tated by Pope's receipt from Hill of a nine-page
analysis, not of any work by Hill himself, but
of Thomson's 'Agamemnon,' on which Pope's
criticism was invited. Pope promised compli-
ance; but—though he continued to send polite
messages to Hill by third parties—'the rest is
silence.' Meanwhile, a year or two earlier, Hill
had found a more congenial friend in Richardson,
soon to be the author of 'Pamela.' The two men

suited each other. Both were letter-writers; both
were valetudinarians; both delighted to discuss the
respective virtues of tar-water and oak-tincture.
Better still, there was no rivalry between them.
Hill was not a fictionist; and Richardson, save in
those hymns of ʿPamela,ʾ where he altered the
Paměla of Sidney and Pope to Paměla, no verseman. Hill, when he admired, was certainly not
lukewarm; and Richardson—as his old friend
Johnson said—ʿcould not be contented to sail
down the stream of reputation, without longing
to taste the froth from every stroke of the oar.ʾ
The acquaintance must have begun about 1736,
but it was not until 1738 that it became confirmed, that being the year in which, after some
mutabilities of fortune, Hill took up his abode at
Plaistow in Essex. His wife had died as far back
as 1731, her death eliciting a more than usually
cordial letter from Pope; but Urania, Minerva,
and Astraea accompanied their father into his
retirement. Of Julius Cæsar, little is recorded;
but it seems clear that he was not a son of whom
his father could be proud.

Plaistow, though then a rural village, did not
prove a desirable residence. The house was large
and old, with a shady, well-grown garden; but
Hill's chief care for the future—besides literature

—was the revival of his former dream of grape-growing in England. He planted 'near a hundred thousand French vines'; but the experiment did not succeed. We hear, indeed, of a bottle of wine sent to Richardson; but what Richardson said of it we do not hear. Clearly, it can scarcely have reached the standard of 'common Sabine'; and Hill might have added, more literally than Horace:

> Mea nec Falernae
> Temperant vites neque Formiani
> Pocula colles—

for he was surprised at his work by an ague, a visitation which speedily ceased to be surprising, since Plaistow was discovered to have a 'moist, malignant Air.' In such conditions, the planning of new groves and grottoes—to say nothing of vineyards—must have gradually palled.

On 8 December 1740 Richardson sent his friend the first two volumes of 'Pamela,' for the kind acceptance of Minerva and Astraea. Urania, by this time, had become the wife of a Mr. Johnson. Whether they guessed the authorship or not, both father and daughters were enraptured. 'Who could have dreamed,' Hill wrote afterwards, in a letter incorporated with the introduction to the second edition, 'who could have

dreamed he should find, under the modest disguise of a novel, all the soul of religion, good
breeding, discretion, good-nature, wit, fancy, fine
thought and morality? . . . It has witchcraft in
every page of it; but it is the witchcraft of passion
and meaning.' In a later letter to Mallet he said
prophetically: 'I am much mistaken in the
promise of his [Richardson's] genius, or 'Pamela'
. . . is but the dawning of the day he is to give
us.' As to the young ladies, they were transported. In July 1741 the flattered little printer
invited the whole family to Salisbury Court; and
in October of the same year Astraea and Minerva
are still assiduously preaching the merits of
'Pamela' and 'Pamela's' author.

Hill extended his admiration to the second part
of 'Pamela,' a view in which he has few followers;
and he even wished to have the 'sweet charmer's
life' stretched to a fifth and sixth volume. During the progress of the forthcoming 'Clarissa,' he
is repeatedly consulted; and he made many practical suggestions, some of which his too-sensitive
friend found extremely embarrassing. Finally, he
allowed himself to be entrapped into the hopeless
task (afterwards performed by E. S. Dallas) of
abridging the 'large, still Book.' He worked
at eight or nine letters with such vigour that

Richardson computed he would reduce the whole
by two-thirds—a reduction to which the unhappy
author, however conscious of his own redundancy,
could by no means reconcile himself. For a time
a coolness ensued, for which Hill was certainly
not to blame; and cordiality was only restored
when the first volumes of the printed novel threw
the whole family into new raptures. Henceforth
Hill prudently confined himself to praise, which
was prolonged to the close. 'I have three girls
around me,' he wrote—'Each a Separate Volume
in her hand, and all their Eyes like a wet flower
in April!'

The enthusiasm of Minerva and Astraea for
'Clarissa' so intoxicated Richardson that he was
unwise enough to solicit their sentiments on the
then-recently issued 'Tom Jones' of Fielding
(1749), which 'Piece,' he pretended, he had
found 'neither Leisure nor Inclination' to read.
They complied in perfect good faith and with
commendable alacrity. They discovered in that
'coarse-titled' book (as Richardson called it) 'a
double Merit, both of Head, and *Heart*.' They
praised its construction. They held that the
events of the fable 'rewarded Sincerity, punished
and exposed Hypocrisy, showed Pity and Be-
nevolence in amiable Lights, and Avarice and

Brutality in very despicable ones.'[1] In short, they blessed when they were expected to have cursed. This was too much for their honoured friend at Fulham, to whom laudation of his rival was gall and wormwood; and the nettled asperity of his rejoinder drew fresh tears, this time of vexation, from the fine eyes of the too-frank young ladies, who were scandalized at having exposed themselves to the suspicion of approving 'a Work of *Evil Tendency*.' Nevertheless they stood to their guns so far as to trust that, on better consideration, Mr. Richardson might come to detect 'a Thread of Moral Meaning' in the peccant Volumes. Richardson watered off into a vague engagement to 'bestow a Reading' on them, should opportunity offer. And this is the last we hear of Minerva and Astraea—those 'Girls of an untittering Disposition.' Aaron Hill himself died in the following year, 8 February 1750, 'at the instant of the earthquake,' and the day before a benefit performance of 'Merope,' which,

---

[1] Miss Brewster prints the entire epistle, though not, she admits, as the discoverer of it. It was first made use of with other Hill letters, in the present writer's 'Fielding' ('Men of Letters' Series), 1883. It is one of the most arresting items in the voluminous (but alas! not luminous) Richardson correspondence at South Kensington.

probably through Mallet, had been commanded
by Frederick, Prince of Wales. He had been ailing for some time. But 'malice domestic' and
'foreign levy,' in the shape of troublesome relatives and tedious Chancery suits, had detained
him too long in the 'terrible marsh-pit'—as
Richardson called it—of Plaistow; and doubtless
shortened his life. He was buried, near his wife,
in the cloisters of Westminster Abbey.

Of his projects and his plays enough has been
said. Of his poetry there is little to add. He
adventured in many kinds: epic, satiric, pin-
daric, lyric. But neither 'Gideon' nor 'The
Fanciad'—neither 'The Northern Star' nor 'The
Art of Acting'—achieved for their writer distinction enough to earn them a place in Mr.
Courthope's 'History of English Poetry' or the
comprehensive selections of Mr. Humphry Ward.
In dictionaries of quotations Hill figures as the
author of a well-known window quatrain:

> *Tender-handed* stroke a *nettle*
> And it *stings* you for your *pains* :
> *Grasp* it, like a *man* of *mettle*,
> And it *soft* as *silk* remains.

(Which also illustrates his morbid fancy for
italics.) He deserves to be remembered as the introducer of Handel to the English operatic stage;

as an earnest advocate of reform when the English theatre was more than ordinarily misruled
and misguided, and as an effective soldier of
English literature at the critical moment when
the dominion of letters was passing from the
Patron to the Public. He was also fairly successful in adapting the tragedies of Voltaire, who,
being a past-master in lucidity, might have taught
him that the adjective is the enemy of the noun.
Even the ready-writing Richardson found his
dear friend's periods 'too munificently adorned!'

A NEW DIALOGUE OF THE DEAD

Mark now, how a plain tale shall put you down.
'Henry IV,' 1st Part, Act ii, Scene iv.

[*It must frequently have occurred to the thoughtful reader that if, in some Lucianic Shadow-Land, authors of reputation could encounter those who compile their lives, the subsequent proceedings might have considerable controversial vivacity —certainly on one side. The following is an attempt to imagine a meeting of this kind between* HENRY FIELDING *and his first biographer,* ARTHUR MURPHY.]

FIELDING.

BY your leave, sir! The light here is as bad as at Bow Street. Did I not hear Dr. Johnson address you just now as 'Mur'?

MURPHY.

My venerated friend sometimes permits himself that familiar contraction. My name is Arthur Murphy—at your service.

263

FIELDING.

Then, Mr. 'Mur,' or Mr. Murphy, you are a murderer.

MURPHY.

Sir, this is extraordinary language.

FIELDING.

Life-making is often life-taking, Mr. Murphy. You wrote—or professed to write—my life. I am Henry Fielding.

MURPHY.

So I conclude. And I assume that you refer to the Essay on your Life and Genius which I prefixed in 1762 to Andrew Millar's edition of your works. Sir, I have a very genuine admiration for your genius; and I thought I had done my best.

FIELDING.

No, sir, you did not do your best. I will not pay you so poor a compliment. Your general estimate—supposing such a piece to be wanted at all—is indeed well enough, though you would have done wisely to reprint entire the preface to the 'Miscellanies' of 1743. But what your admitted digressions on the Middle Comedy of the Greeks, the Machinery of the 'Rape of the

Lock,' Invention, Imitation and the like, have to make with the matter in hand, passes my comprehension. And why drag in Monsieur de Marivaux? However, this is not what I complain of. Our books are fair game; and, provided that you 'nothing extenuate, nor set down aught in malice,' you are welcome to deliver your judgement upon them 'in foro litterario,' according to your parts and capacity. What I do dislike, is your neglect of biographical accuracy. Opinions must inevitably differ; but facts, like rhymes, are stubborn things. You disclaim research, it is true; but you speak at large of the 'prodigious number of materials,' before you—of 'communicating with the ablest and best of the Author's friends.' What you actually do, is to shark together a few disputable and dateless particulars, amounting perhaps to about five per centum of your 'little tract' of ninety-five pages; and from these particulars you proceed to draw out a series of inconsequent conclusions.

MURPHY.

Sir, the existing tradition was in reality but slender. I had scanty opportunity——

FIELDING.

Then you should have looked for more—you

should have made opportunity. I had not been eight years dead. My wife was alive, and probably in the neighbourhood of London; my sister Sally was alive, at Bath. But if you did not wish to consult with 'domestic women' (as I hear a modern critic describes female relatives), there was my old schoolfellow, Lord Lyttelton, in whose 'Dialogues of the Dead' I hear I am mentioned; there was my kind benefactor, Ralph Allen; there was William Hogarth, to whom you did 'obiter' apply—though I don't for a moment believe that master of 'caricatura' ever wanted Patty Collier's scissors to remind him of my nose and chin. Then there was honest Saunders Welch, High Constable of Holborn, who wrote such an excellent description of the 'March to Finchley' for Kit Smart's 'Student.' Welch could have easily given you a sheet of recollections, worth all your 'unconsidered trifles,' for he came with me to Gravesend when I started for Lisbon in the 'Queen of Portugal.' And why did you not get more than the worshipful intelligence that I had compiled two manuscript volumes of Crown Law from my successor at Bow Street, my good brother Jack, who had all my papers; and was, as you seem to have heard, tenderly watching over my family?

Even your publisher, Millar, could have told you
something. Poor Andrew! I hear he left legacies
to my two boys. I wonder whether he ever got
the cyder I bought for him at Torbay!

MURPHY.

I allow that I might possibly have done more
in this direction. But the main point, as it appeared to me, was the exact exhibition of your
literary performances.

FIELDING.

With a seasoning of make-weight erudition
about Attic drama, and the Sylphs and Gnomes
of Mr. Pope—eh, Mr. Murphy? No, sir, it was
not the main point. A critical introduction to a
book is generally about as serviceable as a sermon
before a surloin. What, in the name of Helio-
gabalus, can be the use of commending the food
to the feeder when the final appeal must rest with
his stomach and digestion! On the other hand,
faulty data of a man's life are the kernels around
which inaccuracies accrete to his detriment, and
lapse of time make it difficult to disprove them,
since, as sayeth my Lord Verulam (whom I see
you quote), ' A mixture of a Lie doth ever add
Pleasure.' You must have known, and should have

remembered, that your Essay would be 'ragooed' in reviews like the 'Monthly,' and hashed-up in news-sheets like the 'London Chronicle'—that for years it must be the established biographical authority. And yet you was at no pains to verify the little you gave!

MURPHY.

Your indictment is, to say the least, straightforward. But will you not come to some specific delinquencies?

FIELDING.

Well, it is no easy matter to pick them from their padding. But take one of your earliest sentences. You write that I 'went from Eton to Leyden '——

MURPHY.

And did you not?

FIELDING.

Not as who should say, I went from Newbury to Bath. There was a good deal between—more than three years; and part of the time was occupied . . .

MURPHY.

'Was occupied'?

FIELDING.

By my first love affair. In 1725, when I was eighteen, I was passionately in love with Miss Sarah Andrew, of Lyme Regis. Sir, I should have carried her off 'vi et armis,' if those about her, who doubtless had designs of their own, had not promptly married her to Mr. Rhodes of Modbury. Very possibly she was better off. *He* certainly was, for she had a fine estate at Shapwick; besides 'all the Accomplishments (as the advertisements say) necessary to render the Marriage State truly happy.' But you could hardly know of this, though it is all written in the Register Book of Lyme, when—as I well remember—His Worship 'John Bowdidge, Jun.' was Mayor of that town.

MURPHY.

So far, then, my offence does not seem unpardonable. Will you proceed——

FIELDING.

You go on to say that I studied the civilians 'with a remarkable application.' Remarkable, indeed, though not unusual—since I refrained from studying them at all! When I lodged in that drowsy 'Lugdunum Batavorum,' at the 'Casteel van Antwerpen,' and afterwards at Jan

Oson's, attending 'lectiones' in the class-rooms of the ancient University on the canal, I was enrolled in the 'Album Academicum' as 'Henricus Fielding, Anglus, annor 20, Litt. Stud.' I entered on the 16th of March 1728, being then within a few days of my majority; I was duly mentioned in the recensions of February 1729; and I left in my twenty-second year. Yet, according to you, I returned to London before I was twenty. How did you contrive to make so many blunders in so few lines? Furthermore you say that my first play, 'Love in Several Masques,' was produced when I got back. Would it surprise you to hear, as you must guess from the foregoing dates, that 'Love in Several Masques' was brought out at Drury Lane some weeks before I ever started for Leyden?

MURPHY.

I cannot contradict you, as you are naturally seised of more accurate information. I can only say that I repeated what I could gather.

FIELDING.

Without corroborative evidence? And you date from Lincoln's Inn! Fie! Mr. Murphy. But perhaps one could hardly expect you to make the

journey to Leyden in order to consult the acade-
mic archives. Let us take another point—your
account of my marriage. Here you certainly
throw the reins on what I can only call your
truly Hibernian imagination. You say, in brief,
that 'about that time' (the time I married), when
I had 'not been long a writer for the stage,' I
came, by my mother's death, into a moderate
estate, at East Stour in Dorsetshire, of some two
hundred pounds a year. That having then wedded
a lady with a fortune of under £1,500, I retired
into the country; and 'in less than three years'
wasted all my substance on 'costly yellow liveries,'
horses, hounds and hospitality. But 'mark now,
how a plain tale shall put you down.' The facts
—or some of them—are these. I married on
28 November 1734, at Charlcombe, near Bath.
I had then been a writer for the stage since 1728,
six years. My mother had been dead for more
than sixteen years; and what she had to leave,
an original legacy from my grandfather of £3,000,
had to be shared with four sisters and a brother,
three of whom were, like myself, of age. When
I married my wife she had not a penny, for she
only came into her little fortune a month or two
later, by the death of *her* mother. I was living in
London in February 1735, and I was managing

the French theatre in the Haymarket in the first months of 1736. With respect to my brief intervening life in the country, you are not my confessor; nor is the public any way concerned. But you can scarcely have realized that East Stour (where I had spent my boyhood, and with which I was connected until 1738) was a stone farmhouse, the kitchen being its only 'eating-parlour.' And touching liveries, a gentleman must have his man. I had mine when I left Eton—as timorous Mr. Tucker of Lyme knew to his cost. My wife—both my wives—had their maids; and I carried a footman in livery (a poor creature!) with me to Lisbon. Supposing I had put him in black and yellow (I do not say I did), what were those but the Fielding colours? Surely with such circumstances before you—part at least of which you might have ascertained, you would scarcely have penned your highly decorated story, for which, moreover, you offer no sort of authority.

MURPHY.

Again I cannot contradict you. My story was current, and I saw no reason for not reproducing it.

FIELDING.

With graphic tags and flourishes of your own

no doubt! Confess now that you went no
farther than that granary of gossip, the green-
room of Drury Lane, whence I suspect most of
your information was derived, coupled with faint
praise from those pudding-sleeved pedants, Hurd
and Warburton, whom you compliment so highly.
Were these, by chance, among what you call
the '*ablest and best*' of my friends?

MURPHY.

Sir, if you studied me with such attention, you
must have remarked that My Lord of Gloucester
pays you especial homage.

FIELDING.

Then I misdoubt him. Did you never hear
of the Virgilian commodity known as a Greek
gift? I well remember Warburton at Prior Park,
fulsomely flattering his entertainer. He was
abundantly learned, I grant you . . . Let us, however, return to our muttons. The worst of it is,
these scandals lead to others. Truth gathers
truth tardily; but Error grows like a rolling
snowball. One of your successors improves on
you by saying that I 'determined to show the
rude Squirearchy of Dorset how superior to their
order was the London-bred gentleman.' Nothing
could be more 'gratis dictum'! Further, he has

T

the bad taste to depict my poor Charlotte as a 'fond and foolish' woman 'dazzled by this brief dream of pride and pleasure,' aiding and abetting in all these prodigal excesses! As if anything I have ever written of that best and worthiest and noblest of her sex could possibly justify such an inference! Sir, you did not say these things yourself, yet I cannot but regard you as the begetter of them. Had you not romanced at first, those who followed you would not have romanced afterwards. It is this particular successor of yours who started the cock-and-bull story that I was once a booth-keeper at Bartlemy Fair, a function which, by generous extension, I was later declared to have retained even subsequent to my admission into the Middle Temple. This manifest fabrication would be prospering still had not some one fortunately discovered that the Fielding concerned was not your humble servant at all, but the worthy landlord of the 'Buffalo Tavern' by Bloomsbury Square—an actor who once played Furnish in the 'Miser.' Will you not admit that I have here some cause of complaint?

MURPHY.

I do, though I respectfully decline responsibility for these supplementary misstatements.

FIELDING.

Do you so? Then let me convict you out of your own mouth. 'When his finances were exhausted (you write of me) . . . he would instantly exhibit a farce or a puppet-shew in the Haymarket theatre, which was wholly inconsistent with the profession he had embarked in.' Now, the plain truth is: with exception of 'Miss Lucy in Town' (in the authorship of which I had but a small share), I never exhibited either farce or puppet-show after November 1737, when I adopted the law as a profession. But are not the words I quote (by the way, you contradict them yourself at an earlier stage of your discourse)—are not the words I quote from you a crying illustration of that loose and indigested generalizing which invites the elaboration of unscrupulous pens?—generalizing which is all the more damaging in the case of a man like myself, who, as I have declared repeatedly in print, has suffered shamefully from 'imputed trash, and dulness not his own.'

MURPHY.

You said that I was not your confessor. Permit me to retort that I cannot consent to regard you as mine.

FIELDING.

Which means that my question is unanswerable. But I forbear to prolong this profitless 'examen.' Indeed, you devote so much attention to my 'Genius' ('et quibusdam aliis') that the meagre material of my 'Life' is already run out. I will but note one more blunder which has been extensively copied. If I understand you rightly, you are under the impression that 'Tom Jones' was written after I became a justice of the peace at the end of October 1748. As it was published at the end of February 1749, this would give little more than four months for the invention, preparation and printing of a six volume novel— a feat of fecundity only to be excelled by my esteemed contemporary, Mr. Samuel Richardson, whose remarkable life of Mrs. Pamela Andrews was, we are assured, composed in exactly half that time, namely, from 10 November 1739 to 10 January 1740. 'Prolific Mr. Fielding' as I have been called, I must own, with all humility, that in my case the process was slower. Setting aside the fact that I say expressly at the beginning of my eleventh book that my history 'hath employed some Thousands of Hours in the composing,' I also affirm in my Dedication that it represents 'the Labours of some Years of my

Life.' There was therefore no excuse for implying that I palmed upon the public the hurried product of a period already sufficiently embarrassed by new and exacting municipal duties. But perhaps to suppose that a necessitous writer could possibly linger over a work which he wished to sell, was inconsistent with your preconceived idea of my headlong and hand-to-mouth temperament! To my mind, Mr. Murphy, there is something too much of the preconceived idea in your picture. Out of stage-door scraps and tavern heel-taps you had constructed a dramatist's idea of what I ought to be; and you shrank from submitting your piebald puppet to the touchstone of evidence. Like that great 'biographer' and laureate, Mr. Colley Cibber, you scorned to impoverish your conception by any beggarly exactitude. So the truth must shift for itself! For my own part, I see no sufficient reason for intruding my private doings on the public. As many found out before Pliny: 'No one is wise at all hours.' I make no pretence to freedom from human frailty; and I frankly admit many weaknesses and failures of which, in my calmer moments, I have been ashamed.

> The gods are just, and of our pleasant vices
> Make instruments to scourge us.

I have had *my* lashes—well laid on. And I deserved them. Poor I have been undoubtedly; but
I have also been blessed, like the fellow in Lucian,
with 'friends such as are not to be matched in
Scythia.' More I decline to say, either of accusa-
tion or excuse. But if the full measure of my
culpability is to be traced, 'even to my boyish
years,' that invidious inquisition should surely be
conducted without what you rightly condemn as
the aggravation of facts, or the discolouring of
them by misrepresentation. Nay, you positively
go on to deprecate, in set terms, the drawing
'from premises injuriously established,' and 'with
a pretended reluctance,' of conclusions to the
destruction of my moral character. How you
reconcile these edifying utterances with your own
procedure, I am entirely at a loss to imagine.

MURPHY.

Mr. Fielding, let me say that, so far from——

FIELDING.

Stay—I have but one thing to add. In your
closing words you are good enough to observe
that the 'Journal of a Voyage to Lisbon' reminds
you 'of a person, under sentence of death, jesting
on the scaffold.' Sir, this was ill-said; and it was

not in your brief. Surely it were better 'aequam servare mentem'—to face the inevitable with fortitude—than to whine in useless complaint or bluster in braggart defiance. I had, as I believed, philosophically schooled myself to despise the terrors of death. When I left Ealing I was, to all intents and purposes, a doomed man—a ghastly laughing-stock to the rabble of Redriffe. When I reached Lisbon I rapidly and unexpectedly recovered. My hopes revived. My spirits, which had sunk to the cellar, climbed at once to the top of the house. Had it not been for some miseries with my womankind, I should have felt supremely happy. But it was otherwise decreed——

MURPHY.

Mr. Fielding, on this count, I humbly ask your pardon. If it should ever be my privilege to return to the world in any capacity that involves the holding of a pen, I will endeavour to do justice to the facts of your biography——

FIELDING.

Nay, sir, I absolve you. 'Semel emissum volat irrevocabile verbum!' Leave me severely alone: 'twill be best for us both. Maybe some later writer will try his hand at my rehabilitation, and

clear me—as much as he can. Moreover, English
fiction has, I am told, made vast strides since the
days when I first sketched, in the ' Preface' to
' Joseph Andrews'—perhaps a little 'ad hoc'—my
plan of a comic Epic-Poem in Prose; and it is
quite possible that what I then deemed my ' new
Province of Writing' may now require radical
revision. Farewell! you are forgiven. I think I
see yonder my old friend Ralph Allen, whom I, a
younger man, once fondly thought to survive.
But Goodness is your true ' Elixir Vitæ' !

NOTES

TO

'A NEW DIALOGUE OF THE DEAD'

'*On doit des égards aux vivants, on ne doit que la vérité aux morts.*'—VOLTAIRE, *Preface to '*Œdipe.*'*

'*He that writes the Life of another is either his friend or his enemy.*'—JOHNSON, '*Idler,*' No. 84.

'*There is no need* [*observed Don Quixote*] *of recording events which do not change or affect the truth of a history, if they tend to bring the hero of it into contempt.*'—DON QUIXOTE, *Pt. ii, ch. iii, Ormsby's translation.*

NOTES TO 'A NEW DIALOGUE OF THE DEAD'

NOTE 1, p. 263.—AS BAD AS AT BOW STREET. Bow Street Police Office, Fielding's last town residence. It was destroyed by the mob in the riots of '80. (See *ante*, pp. 139, 150.)

NOTE 2, p. 263.—'MUR.' 'Johnson had a way of contracting the names of his friends; as Beauclerk, Beau; Boswell, Bozzy; Langton, Lanky; Murphy, Mur; Sheridan, Sherry' (Hill's 'Boswell's Johnson,' 1887, ii, 258).

NOTE 3, p. 265.—MONSIEUR DE MARIVAUX. Fielding was admittedly familiar with the 'Paysan Parvenu,' and the 'Histoire de Marianne'; but we have the well-known Whistler-Velazquez anecdote to warrant us in supposing that he would not have welcomed a comparison with Marivaux.

NOTE 4, p. 265.—IN FORO LITTERARIO. Fielding uses this expression in 'Tom Jones,' Bk. xi, Ch. i.

NOTE 5, p. 265.—FACTS, LIKE RHYMES, ARE STUBBORN THINGS. Cp. 'Amelia,' Bk. viii, Ch. v.

NOTE 6, p. 266.—EIGHT YEARS DEAD. Murphy wrote in 1762; and Fielding died 8 October 1754, aged forty-eight.

NOTE 7, p. 266.—MY WIFE WAS ALIVE. His second wife (Mary Daniel) survived until the 11th of March 1802. But, it should be added, she may well have known little of her husband's life previous to his first marriage.

283

NOTE 8, p. 266.—MY SISTER SALLY. Sarah Fielding died April 1768, and is buried in Charlcombe Church, near Bath.

NOTE 9, p. 266.—DOMESTIC WOMEN. 'Authors rarely acquaint domestic women with the progress of their writings' (Advertisement to the 2nd edition of Nichols's 'Biographical Anecdotes of William Hogarth,' 1782. The writer was George Steevens (see *ante*, pp. 204-6). We are here (with Lyttelton), assuming that '*the* Dead *are supposed to know what has past, in subsequent times . . . as well as their own*' (Preface to 'Dialogues of the Dead,' 1760, p. v).

NOTE 10, p. 266.—IN WHOSE DIALOGUES OF THE DEAD, I AM MENTIONED. Not, however, by Lyttelton. The reference to Fielding is in the third of three papers contributed to his Lordship's work by the 'Queen of the Blue Stockings,' Mrs. Elizabeth Montagu. They were her first literary effort.

NOTE 11, p. 266.—RALPH ALLEN. Ralph Allen died in June 1764, nine years after Fielding.

NOTE 12, p. 266.—WILLIAM HOGARTH. Hogarth died 26 October 1764. As to his sketch of Fielding and the Collier legend, see Nichols's 'Biographical Anecdotes' of the painter, 1781, p. 131, and John Ireland's 'Hogarth Illustrated,' 1798, iii, 291.

NOTE 13, p. 266.—HONEST SAUNDERS WELCH. Welch died in October 1784. His article in the 'Student' appeared in vol. ii, p. 162.

NOTE 14, p. 266.—MY GOOD BROTHER JACK. John Fielding, Fielding's half-brother, and later Sir John, died in September 1780.

NOTE 15, p. 267.—YOUR PUBLISHER, MILLAR. Andrew Millar died in 1768. His legacies to William and Allen Fielding are mentioned in the D.N.B. account of him. As to the 'cyder,' see 'A Fielding Find' ('At Prior Park,' 1912, p. 134).

NOTE 16, p. 267.—AS SAYETH MY LORD VERULAM. In his first Essay, 'Of Truth.'

NOTE 17, p. 268.—YOU WAS. Fielding, with other writers, frequently uses this where only one person is concerned.

NOTE 18, p. 269.—MY FIRST LOVE-AFFAIR. See 'Athenæum' for 2 June 1883, or Appendix No. 1 to the writer's 'Fielding' in the 'Men of Letters' series, 1907.

NOTE 19, p. 269.—ALL THE ACCOMPLISHMENTS. This was a 'cliché' of eighteenth-century journalese at which Fielding was fond of poking fun.

NOTE 20, p. 269.—STUDIED THE CIVILIANS. See, for the authority for this paragraph, 'Macmillan's Magazine' for April 1907, and the writer's 'Fielding' *ut supra.*

NOTE 21, p. 271.—YOUR ACCOUNT OF MY MARRIAGE. See 'Fielding,' *ut supra*, and for additional particulars Miss G. M. Godden's 'Henry Fielding,' 1910.

NOTE 23, p. 272.—THE FIELDING COLOURS. See Mr. Keightley's 'Postscript' in 'Fraser's Magazine' for June 1858 to his Fielding articles.

NOTE 23, p. 273.—ONE OF YOUR SUCCESSORS. This reference is to Mr. Frederick Lawrence's 'Life of Fielding,' 1855, a sincere and conscientious study, but somewhat given to filling gaps by guesswork.

NOTE 24, p. 274.—SOME ONE FORTUNATELY DIS- COVERED. Mr. Frederick La Treille, in 'Notes and Queries' for 1875 (Fifth Series, iii, 502), con- clusively identified the Fielding of Bartlemy Fair, with a minor player called Timothy Fielding, afterwards landlord of the Buffalo Tavern, by Bloomsbury Square. Oddly enough one of his parts was that of a 'trading justice,' Quorum, in Coffey's 'Beggar's Wedding.'

NOTE 25, p. 275.—REPEATEDLY IN PRINT. E.g., in the Preface to the 'Miscellanies,' 1743, and the Preface to the Second Edition of 'David Simple,' 1744.

NOTE 26, p. 275.—IMPUTED TRASH. Pope, Prologue to the 'Satires,' l. 351.

NOTE 27, p. 276.—PROLIFIC MR. FIELDING. He was so styled in the 'Prompter' of Aaron Hill, No. 29.

NOTE 28, p. 277.—AS MANY FOUND OUT BEFORE PLINY. The quotation is from Pliny, 7, 40, 2.

NOTE 29, p. 277.—THE GODS ARE JUST. 'King Lear,' Act v, Sc. 3. The modern rendering is 'plague us.' But it was 'scourge' in Fielding's Shakespeare; and we know, by the 'Journey from this World to the Next,' that Fielding had no great passion for variants. 'When two Meanings of a Passage can in the least ballance our Judgements which to prefer'—he says pleasantly—'I hold it matter of unquestionable Certainty that neither is worth a Farthing.'

NOTE 30, p. 278.—THE FELLOW IN LUCIAN. This illustration, but not its application, is borrowed from another lover of the Samosatene, the late Sidney T. Irwin of Clifton College. In 1894 Mr. Irwin published a version of 'Six Dialogues of Lucian,' with a delightful Introduction. Here he had the advantage of Fielding, who got no farther than 'proposals to translate' (with 'Mr. Abraham Adams') the author upon whom, as he affirmed, he had formed his own style.

NOTE 31, p. 278.—EVEN TO MY BOYISH YEARS. In the 'Jacobite's Journal,' Fielding complains sadly that his enemies have traced his impeachment 'even to his boyish Years.'

NOTE 32, p. 278.—THE AGGRAVATION OF FACTS. 'Where suppression is required, useful auxiliary guidance is offered by Cicero's wise dictum that when you are debarred from saying all that is true, you must say nothing that is false, or that conveys a false impression' (Sir Sidney Lee on Biography in the 'Nineteenth Century and After,' for December 1912, p. 1162).

NOTE 33, p. 279.—THE RABBLE OF REDRIFFE, *i.e.*, Rotherhithe, whence Fielding embarked for Portugal, and, in his own words, 'ran the gauntlope . . . through rows of sailors and watermen, few of whom failed of paying their compliments to me, by all manner of insults and jests on my misery' ('Journal of a Voyage to Lisbon,' 'World's Classics,' 1907, p. 29).

NOTE 34, p. 279.—MY SPIRITS. See Fielding's last (?) letter in 'A Fielding Find' ('At Prior Park,' 1912, p. 145).

NOTE 35, p. 279.—SEMEL EMISSUM VOLAT IRREVO-CABILE VERBUM. Horace, Epp. i, 18, l. 71.

NOTE 36, p. 280.—MY 'NEW PROVINCE OF WRITING.' 'Tom Jones,' Book ii, Ch. 1.

GENERAL INDEX

N.B.—*The titles of articles are in capitals*

U

Cadell, Thomas, 90.

Cagliostro, 162.

Calverley, C. S., 78 n.

Camillus, Hill's, 233.

Campbell, Archibald, 66, 67.

Carriera, Andrea, 5, 8.

Carriera, Angela, 7.

Carriera, Giovanna or Giovannina, 7, 9, 26, 27, 30.

Carriera, Rosalba, 1-31.

Caroline of Naples, 174.

Carteret, Lord, 207, 231.

Casali, The Chevalier, 145.

Catherine II, 179.

Cave, Edward, 210, 216, 221, 222, 224.

Cave, Richard, 224.

Caylus, Comte de, 17, 28.

'Cease Rude Boreas,' 70.

Chaillu, Paul du, 32.

Chaloner, Mr., 2.

Chambers, Sir R., 35.

Chanclos, Countess Josepha de, 173.

Chanterenne, Mme. Hilaire, 170, 172.

Chapelle, Count de la, 188 n.

Chapone, Mrs., 126.

Charenton, Reviews at, 15.

Charlcombe, 271.

Charles VI, 26, 30.

Charles, The Archduke, 173, 174.

Charlotte, Queen, 123.

Chartres, Duc de, 21.

Chenevix, Mrs., 119.

Chocolatière, La, 31.

Churchill, Charles, 89.

Chute, John, 2, 3.

Cibber, Susannah Maria, 245.

Cicero, Conyers Middleton's, 208.

Cicero on Biography, 287.

Clarissa, Richardson's, 258, 259.

Clarke, Rev. James Stanier, 65.

Clement of Saxony, Prince, 172.

Cleone, Dodsley's, 72.

Clerke, Sir Philip Jennings, 53.

Cléry, J. C. H., 169, 183.

Clinton, Henry, Earl of Lincoln, 2, 3.

Cobbler Poets, 199.

Cocchi, Antonio, 3.

Colleen Bawn, Boucicault's, 32.

Collignon, Chevalier, 188 n.

Collier, Arthur, 39 n.

Dorset, Earl of Dorset, 68.
Doubleday, Thomas, 128.
Down Hall, Prior's, 97.
Drouet, 'Old Dragoon,'
171 n.
Dubois, Abbé, 22.
Duck, Stephen, 217 n.
Dudley, Lord, 135.
Duick, John, 220.
Dumouriez, Gen., 171.
Dunciad, Pope's, 252.
Duplessi-Bertaux, 172 n.
Dupplin, Lord, 112.

EARLY YEARS OF MME.
ROYALE, THE, 164-194.
East Stour, Fielding at, 271.
Edgeworth, Abbé, 181,
183, 185, 186.
Elfrid, Hill's, 238, 243.
Elizabeth, Archduchess,
173.
Elizabeth, Empress, 26, 31.
Elizabeth, Princess, 166.
Ellis, Welbore, 135.
Elstob, Elizabeth, 110, 111.
Emma, Miss Austen's, 65 n.
Enghien, Duc d', 174.
Erskine, Thomas, 157, 158,
159.
*Essay on Life and Genius of
Fielding*, Murphy's, 264.

Evelina, Miss Burney's, 51,
52.

'Fairly, Col.,' 63, 64, 83,
86.
Fair Quaker of Deal, Charles
Shadwell's, 239.
Falconer, Mrs., 93.
FALCONER'S SHIPWRECK,
63-94.
Falconer, William, 63-
94.
Fatal Extravagance, Hill's,
241.
Fatal Vision, Hill's, 241.
Faulkner, the lapidary,
113.
Fermor, Lady Sophia, 2
Fiançailles de Mme. Royale,
Pimodan's, 165.
Fielding, Henry, 52, 160,
210, 263-280.
Fielding, Mrs. (Mary
Daniel), 266.
Fielding, Sarah, 266.
Fielding, Timothy, 274,
286.
Fielding, Sir John, 139,149,
150, 266.
Fille de Louis XVI, La,
Lenôtre's, 164.
Flint, Bet., 53.

Quin, James, 111, 244.
Quixote, Don, on Biography," 282.

Raimbach, Abraham, 143.
Rambler, Johnson's, 226.
Ramillies, loss of the, 73, 77 n.
Rawlinson, Dr. R., 212.
Rayner, Mr., 231.
Reed, Isaac, 202, 204.
Reliquæ Baxterianæ, 207.
Remedies, Old, 106-107:
Reynolds, Sir J., 54, 55, 56.
Rhodes, Mr. Ambrose, 269.
Ricci, Sebastian, 25.
Richardson, Samuel, 51, 209, 226, 251, 257, 276.
Richardson and Hill, 256.
Richmond, Duke of, 16.
Richmond, Duchess of, 16.
Ridgway, James, 159.
Rinaldo, Hill's, 240.
RIOTS, THE GORDON, 129-163.
Ritchie, Lady, 33.
Roberts, Mr. Henry D., 4 n.
Robespierre, F. M., 168, 169.
Robinson, Elizabeth, 108.

Rodmond in *The Shipwreck*, 84.
Roman Revenge, Hill's, 246.
Rosalba Carriera, 1-31.
ROSALBA'S JOURNAL, 1-31.
Rosamond, Addison's, 240.
Roundabout Papers, Thackeray's, 32.
Rousseau, Jean Jacques, 119.
Royal George, 87.
Royale, Madame, 164-194.
Rubens, P. P., 15.

Saint Sulpice, 13.
St. George's Fields, 132.
St. John, Lord, 135.
St. John's Gate, 216, 217.
Salusbury, Miss Hester Lynch, 38, 39.
Salusbury, Mr., 38.
Salusbury, Mrs., 38, 45, 46 n.
Salusbury, Sir Thomas, 38.
Sandwich, Lord, 130, 138.
Sandys, Lord, 55.
San Roch, Procession du Pain at, 15.
Sartori, Felicita, 26.
Savage, Richard, 52, 220.
Savile, Sir George, 131, 138, 146.